The One-Minute Meeting™

How To Speak Without Fear, Inspire Any Audience, And Conduct Time-Effective Meetings

by
Omar Periu

"Whether you are planning your first meeting or brushing up on meeting etiquette and "how-to's," The One Minute Meeting will answer your questions. Omar Periu writes in his easy-to-understand, enjoyable style successful, productive meetings."

Zig Ziglar, Author

"The One Minute Meeting is a must read for every executive business person, entrepreneur and anyone who must make and attend meetings. Omar has made the idea of a business meeting fun again."

Dr. Earl Mindell, Author/Nutritionist

"Omar is one of the most inspiring, entertaining, and motivating speakers in business today. Learn from him, the specific ways to raise your standards of presenting meetings. This book is a must for anyone who stands in front of an audience."

Joe Walsh, CEO Yellow Book USA

"No doubt about it! This book is the best I have EVER read on the subject of Meetings. Great information for everyone connected with the industry. Don't miss it. In fact, buy a bunch and use them as business gifts, your clients will truly appreciate!"

Dottie Walters, Walters International Speakers Bureau Speak&GrowRich

"Omar has done it again, he has captured winning formulas for business success and explained them in a simple and practical context that gives the reader a road map to accomplish greater professional and personal success."

Reggie Vaughn, AVP of Retail Development, Southeast Toyota

"The One Minute Meeting has been a fantastic tool for my business. When speaking to a group, effective communication is key. Omar has mastered this and has created a simple and easy to follow book that is filled with valuable pointers that can help everyone. We will use this great book for years to come!"

Rick Capadonna, CEO Carico

"Every leader knows that to reach the top, you have to acquire the ability to create and present a great meeting. The One Minute Meeting is a needed addition to your managers tool box. Following Omar's advice will help you master the skills required to be an effective communicator and a great presenter!"

Scott Patterson, President and CEO Trinity Holdings, Inc.

"I highly recommend this book to any business professional who wants to enhance their ability to communicate with clarity and proficiency to individuals or groups. I have studied many books on speaking skills and Omar's book is head and shoulders above the rest."

Tom Vaught, Vice President Fitness USA

"The One Minute Meeting is today's most useful, comprehensive, and the best book on meetings I have ever read. It's packed with invaluable content and advice for everyone from the beginner to the professional speaker. What a terrific book!"

Jim Piccolo - Chancellor, Nouveau Riche Corporation

"The One Minute Meeting is an outstanding guide to public speaking, written by a master speaker. The advice, practical techniques, and strategies contained in this book will be valuable to anyone who is interested in making their presentations more compelling."

Charles Biondo, Regional VP/Sprint Business Solutions

"What a simple and empowering book! Anyone interested in personal and professional growth can really benefit from The One Minute Meeting. When you need to speak in a one-on-one discussion; or in a small to large group presentation... this book will help you achieve your key objectives!"

Marty Matthews President, Vital Age International, Inc.

The One Minute Meeting™

Published by
Omar Periu International, Inc.
P. O. Box 812470
Boca Raton, FL 33481
www.OmarPeriu.com

Library of Congress Cataloging-in Publication Data
available upon request.
ISBN: 0-9704368-1-5
1. Presentations and 2. Meetings
Printed in the United States of America
First Edition

For sales inquiries and special prices for bulk quantities, please contact Omar Periu International, Inc. at 888-777-4519, or write to the address in the back of this book.

Table of Contents

This book is dedicated to
my wife Helen,
who inspires me
to continue the journey
to live my dream of helping others.
To my Princess Alexandra
and my little King Maxwell,
who motivate me on a daily basis
with their love.

ABOUT OMAR PERIU

Omar Periu is a powerful man with a truly remarkable life story. He's more than a motivator; his peers refer to him as *"The Motivational Teacher."* Possessing an indefinable quality of magnetism, Omar's educational seminars raise audience awareness to a higher level. Although the terms *"dynamic," "high energy,"* and *"super achiever"* all describe Omar Periu as he is today, they aren't exactly the words that portrayed the results accomplished earlier in his career.

Omar and his family fled Castro's regime when he was only seven years old. They arrived in Miami with no money, no relatives or friends in America and nothing but the clothes on their backs. Thus began Omar's journey of success in the land of freedom and opportunity.

Enduring the taunting of other children, the cold winters of Illinois and the language barrier, Omar made a conscious and deliberate decision to pursue his dream of personal achievement. His father, reading from a tattered Spanish copy of Dale Carnegie's book, *"How to Win Friends and Influence People,"* taught Omar one of the greatest lessons in life. *"It doesn't matter who you are, where you;re from or what color you are, you can do anything you put your mind to."*

Initially, Omar had a limited understanding and little success with the sales and leadership process and its outcome. However, after studying the masters and observing the difference between the performance of top salespeople and succesful entrepreneurs compared to those barely squeaking by, Omar developed **The Investigative Selling Principles.** Implementing those investigative principles in his own career, it wasn't long before Omar became one of the top professionals in his field. Before the age of 31, he was a self-made millionaire, owning some of the most profitable health clubs and sports medicine facilities in the United States. From his modest beginning as a take-it-on-the-chin salesperson, Omar knew the pain of sales rejection and failure. He also discovered the high of mastering sales presentations and sophisticated closing skills. Most importantly, he is now teaching these unique investigative principles to salespeople, managers, and entrepreneurs all over the world. Like Omar's experience, having internalized these principles, his students are now reporting their greatest sales triumphs ever!

His tremendous success led him into sales management, and he has devoted the last 20 years to the training and development of sales and leadership professionals. Since that time, Omar has provided high-impact instruction on the topic of sales management and sales leadership throughout the world with live seminars, cassettes, CD's, coaching, mentoring and in-house video training systems.

He has personally recruited, hired, trained, and managed both inside telephone-based sales associates and retail/field salespeople, as well as customer service professionals. Furthermore, since sales leadership is an ever-changing discipline, he felt it was imperative that he kept his finger on the pulse by currently managing his own corporations and sales professionals on a daily basis. This hands-on, in-the-trenches sales and sales management leadership has made Omar one of the top sales management and leadership trainers in the world.

Omar's content is fresh and inspiring, his presentations impeccable, and his story unforgettable. He is now referred to as the number one "how to" sales and leadership trainer in America, a world-traveled speaker who has spent over a decade educating salespeople, managers and entrepreneurs worldwide. He has trained more than two million people in more than two-thirds of the Fortune 500 companies, teaching over 5,000 seminars, workshops and training programs in his career. He is a member of The National Speakers Association and has been inducted into the prestigious International Platform Association.

Through hard work and determination, Omar became recognized as a highly professional salesperson, sales leader and entrepreneur. You can do the same. He is committed to helping people like you to achieve their full potential through mastering *"The Investigative Selling Principles™"* and *"From Management to Leadership Techniques™"* and now this new, exciting book *"The One Minute Meeting™."* To quote Omar's philosophy -- *"Success is in the moment - so make each moment count!"*

ACKNOWLEDGEMENTS

There are many people who made this book possible. Their knowledge, inspiration, dedication and hard work have made The One Minute Meeting a dream come true.

To my wife Helen, for her support when my life's passion takes me away.

To my children, who let me experience things through them, you are a true inspiration.

A special thanks to my parents, who have always made sure that I knew that I was destined for greatness.

I would like to thank Dan Baldwin for his outstanding writing. Your creativity and willingness to go the extra mile has helped me and others receive more from this book.

To John Martin, for his countless hours working on the layout to make sure that my words are presented in an easy-to-read and interesting format.

To Chris Bongart and Kelly Turner for a cover design that creatively captures the book's essence

To Ryan Jordan, for her dedication. I don't know what I would do without you. Thank you for making sure that everything is outstanding.

Last, but not least, I would like to thank all of my mentors, especially Zig Ziglar, Tom Hopkins, Tom Murphy and friends in my industry that have taught and mentored me both professionally and personally. I have become who I am because of your invested support.

I wish you great Success!

FOREWORD

Life is a seminar. Life is a series of meetings to master. (My friend Omar's) The One Minute Meeting™, How to Speak Without Fear, Inspire Any Audience, and Conduct Time-Effective Meetings, techniques will make your life infinitely better, richer, more satisfying and most of all will get you the results you want faster. If you're objective is to do more in less time and maximize your results –reading, absorbing and using the brilliance in this book is a must.

Omar is a great and inspiring speaker –leader. So he teaches by example. His modeling and insights will instantly propel your success in meetings. Best of all, he will finish by teaching you how to make fear your friend, ally and assistant in conquering all the many meetings in your future. Enjoy this life changing book.

Mark Victor Hansen
Co-Author The One Minute Millionaire and
Co-Founder Chicken Soup for the Soul

INTRODUCTION

I have planned, organized, set-up, attended, conducted, managed, co-managed (and, yes) ducked, dodged and avoided more meetings than I can count and for more years than I'd like to count. People who attend meetings generally fall into three distinct categories.

First, there are the people who do not want to attend meetings. They perceive meetings as a waste of time, as non-productive assignments, or even as actions counter-productive to the goals of the organization. These folks may be highly skilled and very talented, but their negative attitude automatically blunts their effectiveness.

A second group really loves to attend meetings, but for all the wrong reasons. They see meetings as an easy way to get out of work while making the impression that they are actually getting something accomplished. Obviously, as a meeting leader this isn't a description of your "dream team."

The third group, and I am a member of that group, sees meetings not only as a necessary element of modern life, but as a productive tool in reaching important goals. That's the key - knowing your goals and doing everything possible through the medium of a meeting to achieve them. That is what I call intent. Whether you're selling a new product to your sales force or a marketing program to the company, the meeting has intent. Intent is the "something" that you want to accomplish.

Congratulations. By picking up, studying and putting into practice the principles of this book you're joining an elite fraternity of progressive CEOs, presidents, top executives, managers and meeting enthusiasts. Meetings do not have to sap the energy of the organization or its people. In fact done correctly, meetings can be exciting, productive, and empowering tools of modern corporate, industrial and organizational practice. Yes, meetings can even be fun.

Meetings are necessary tools of success. You will encounter them everywhere and they will not go away. If you're involved in leading an organization, anything from the local automobile dealership to international conglomerates, you will be attending meetings. Many of you will be called upon to speak within them and some will be given the responsibility for planning and managing meetings. If these "tools of success" are so important and inevitable, why not do them in a way that we get the most from our efforts? Why don't we start earning a feeling of accomplishment from our meetings?

The biggest problem with most meetings and with those who plan and execute them is a lack of focus on intent. What are we supposed to be doing in this meeting, anyway? What's our real goal and are we achieving it or are we moving in the wrong direction? The failure of most meetings is directly related to the simple phrase -"specific intent." "Specific Intent" is the results you intend to achieve from your meetings. If you do not have specific intent and if you do not aggressively pursue your specific intent, then your meeting will be reflective of that pre-conceived attitude.

I wrote this book as the result of my clients asking me about all the different ways you achieve your specific intent. How do you speak effectively at meetings? How can you overcome the fear of speaking? What tools should I use to enhance my presentation? How should I look and act? How do I motivate, inspire, educate and keep them interested at the meeting while at the same time making sure they have fun during the process? This book is designed to show you just how to do that and more. It is segmented into two parts: time effective meetings and speaking without fear. In this book you will learn how to plan, organize, manage and address great meetings. You'll see how to turn those dull, non-productive exercises into dynamic vehicles for change and accomplishment. I know. I've done everything you could possibly do wrong when it comes to meetings. More important, I've learned from every one of those mistakes. I've studied hard. I've researched the materials, I've spoken to the experts, and I've conducted my own experiments. I have spoken to more than 2,000,000 people and have given more than 5,000 presentations. I understand meetings and I know how to speak at them effectively and efficiently while managing fear.

And I'm here to help you.

You hold in your hand the guidebook to the essentials of managing and speaking at great meetings. Here's what to do, how to do it well, and why. This book is designed for the CEO who faces a board of international directors, the owner of his or her own company, vice presidents of corporations, department heads, managers and sales managers, and anyone else who wants to conduct great meetings. In short, this book is for you. This is a platform from which you can show the committee, the department, the company, the conglomerate - the world - that you are a great meeting manager and an outstanding speaker. Are you ready to speak without fear, inspire any audience, and conduct time-effective meetings at any time?

I thought so.

Then let's get started.

Part I.

Time Effective Meetings

1

"Today a reader, tomorrow a leader."

W. Fusselman

Meet The One-Minute Meeting

Colin Powell said you can judge a pro by what he (or she) wants to know after they "know it all." To be a great leader and an effective communicator, you must be a great reader. You must want to know more than you know. I've dedicated my life to being a student of people so I can help people become more powerful and more eloquent leaders. A considerable portion of those efforts has been directed toward training people to conduct and speak at meetings. I mean great meetings, not those tepid, washed-out, ineffectual corporate exercises in futility we all dread.

Part One of this book focuses on conducting great meetings. As much as possible, a great speaker controls his or her speaking environment. Here we'll see how to plan, organize and manage a great speaking environment. Do you want to conduct great meetings? Do you want to become a great speaker? Do you want to be a great corporate leader? If your answer is a resounding "yes," then keep reading. Together, we'll get there.

Meetings are a fact of modern life. No one is immune. Even if you avoid the boardroom, you'll still find yourself in the meeting room, offices, break rooms and the hallways - meeting. Many of us will be involved in numerous meetings for numerous groups throughout our lives. Doesn't it make good sense to become so proficient that we become experts?

Whenever Two Or More Are Gathered

Meetings are an integral part of our lives, yet how many of us have received training at conducting and speaking at meetings? Sadly, the answer is "very few."

I have the honor of addressing audiences that range from military to corporate to the general public. I have seen it all, the good and the bad. I have listened as CEOs, presidents, officers, managers and others bore their audiences with monotone speeches, unorganized and unimaginative words, inappropriate stories, and humiliating attempts at humor. I've seen owners of large organizations "choke" and start sweating before addressing an audience. I've seen leaders start crying in front of thousands of people because they couldn't control their fear of speaking and I've seen them come apart at the most embarrassing moment possible.

My goal is to see that you never have a bad meeting or speech again. You can become an outstanding speaker. You can conduct powerful time-effective and motivational meetings. You can inspire, educate and entertain others. You can conduct meetings and give speeches that will motivate people toward your desired action. Your road to meeting and speaking greatness starts right here, right now.

What is a meeting, anyway? Well, I like the definition provided in the Bible. Whenever "two or more are gathered" for a specific purpose, you have a meeting. With that specific purpose in mind, and realizing that you and I are now "gathered together," let's open this session with a look at the way we conduct meetings and how we can make the process more efficient, productive and, dare I say it, even fun.

What's Wrong Today

There is a lot wrong with the majority of today's meetings. Here is a short list of challenges I've seen and experienced over the years. Do any of these sound familiar to you?

• ***Lack of focus.*** Everyone comes to the meeting with his or her own agenda. Serious issues are given little attention or are even ignored as lesser issues dominate the conversation.

• ***Poor leadership.*** The group leader does not have to rule the meeting as a dictator, but has to exhibit some management skills. Too many of our leaders allow their meetings to disintegrate into little more than free-for-alls.

• *Absence of preparation.* This is primarily due to faulty leadership, although plenty of committee members arrive unprepared. A meeting isn't a "New Age" experience of folks communing. It is, or should be, intent driven and therefore careful planning is essential.

• *Lack of an agenda.* Every meeting must have an agenda, even if there is only one topic under discussion. The agenda is an essential element of that careful planning I just mentioned.

• *Going off the reservation.* What good is a meeting agenda if the leader allows the attendees to bring up their own issues? Once the agenda (intent) is established, it must be followed to the letter. Yes, there may be exceptions to the rule, but they should be few and very far between.

• *Timing challenges.* How many of us have attended meetings that started late and then ran long? If I were at a presentation right now, I'd be looking at a sea of raised hands. Timing is primarily a function of leadership. A leader respects his or her team by starting on time, controlling the process throughout the meeting, and then by ending as scheduled.

• *Meeting just to have a meeting.* How many of us have gone to an unnecessary meeting simply because "we've always done it that way?" Ah, there's that sea of hands again. Folks, if there's no reason to have a meeting, then don't tie up all of that valuable time and talent. If there's no real intent, then there's no real meeting.

• *No follow through.* Too many meetings seem to be dedicated more to the process than to the successful results of that process. The attitude seems to be, "Well, we've had our meeting, so now we don't have to do anything." Without tangible results, people feel their time has been wasted and rightly so.

• *Unnecessary distractions.* The meeting leader takes a phone call during the meeting. Someone walks in expecting to be at another meeting. Suddenly the flow is interrupted and it takes fifteen or twenty minute for everyone to get back the momentum. The meeting drags on and is no longer time effective.

One of the worst distractions occurs when key players walk in and out of a meeting. If the meeting is important enough for them attend, then they should attend. Moving in and out sends all kinds of negative messages. The act demeans the meeting and those present.

Ringing, beeping, buzzing, music-playing cell phones are another major distraction. I always ask everyone to turn off their cell phones at the beginning of a session. I also ask that no one leaves until the scheduled breaks. I explain that my program builds. Each stage is important because it sets up and leads into the next. Missing any part of the program would be like reading a book and skipping a key chapter.

• *Unrealistic expectations.* If everyone believes that the meeting will never achieve its stated goal, then the attention span, excitement level, and commitment of the participants will result in a lack of progress. The team leader must achieve a balance between seeking the impossible and "reaching a little higher than your grasp." The former is, as stated, impossible, and the latter is the definition of leadership.

• *Dominating personalities/non-participating personalities.* Some people speak too much while others don't speak at all. It's the leader's job to manage the meeting according to the agenda. Sometimes that involves squelching a blowhard and other times you have to coax comments with the skill of a fly fisherman after a swift trout in a flowing stream.

There are other challenges, but I think you get the point. If you'll read and open your minds to the words in this book, I'll show you how your meetings can be vastly improved. So, let's start moving in that direction. All in favor, say Aye!

The Ayes have it.

> *"Things in which mediocrity is insupportable - poetry, music, painting, public speaking."*
> La Bruyere

Types Of Meetings

Meetings fall into all kinds of classifications. You might be conducting a simple one-on-one with another manager or directing a world-wide video conference involving hundreds of individuals. The meeting could be a regular Monday morning executive round table or a spur of the moment "we've got to do something now" crisis or opportunity. Regardless of how it may appear, all meetings fall into certain categories. Let's take a quick look at each one.

Scheduled Meetings

Scheduled meetings are usually set up to monitor or enhance the regular operations of the organization. Sales meetings, regularly scheduled committee meetings, and board meetings are examples. Often their purpose is informational. With solid preparation, these meetings can be effective and mercifully brief. For example, why invest the valuable time of committee members on a subject that can be handled more efficiently elsewhere? A lot of energy can be saved if Julie says to Dave, "I'll get together with you on that after the meeting." Try to schedule these meetings on the same day and at the same time of the week or month. Warning - generally, a scheduled meeting should not be allowed to drift into other arenas, such as problem solving or brainstorming.

Opportunity/Crisis Meeting

Some things just won't wait till first thing Monday morning. The sudden appearance of a new client in the marketplace, a proposed change in compensation for the sales force, the need for major capital investments, or reviewing the resume of a top executive suddenly available for employment are examples.

This type of meeting requires a decision and a plan of action. Key players must be involved, but only key players. Rapid evaluation and decision making is critical and the meeting can't be bogged down with unnecessary interruptions from people who feel a need to "contribute" even if they have nothing to say. A strong leader is needed to make sure the group retains its focus. Again, a successful meeting is all about intent.

Problem Solving Meetings

A problem is not necessarily a sudden crisis or a new opportunity. Often there's a lot of advance notice. For example, the CEO is retiring in two years, the plant is relocating from Chicago to Cheyenne, or new technology is endangering the success of your product line. The problem solving meeting is often a series of meetings that may continue for months or even years. Attendees, therefore, should have ample time for research and preparation for each session. The focus should be on providing and evaluating various solutions to the problem at hand and then making specific recommendations.

Decision Meetings

The group has just been handed recommendations from a problem-solving committee. What next? The group must evaluate those recommendations and then make a decision as to which one to implement. Such a decision may be made in a single meeting or may require a number of meetings over time depending upon the organization's timetable, resources, market demands and other factors.

Warning - too many people in today's organizations are fearful of making any kind of decision. They find the perpetual committee meeting a warm and fuzzy comfort zone. When a decision is needed, be sure to set a specific date for everyone to say "aye" or "nay."

Implementation Meetings

These meetings are called to answer the question, "How do we get from here to there?" Again, there's always a danger of the meeting becoming a comfort zone. Avoid this by assigning responsibility and authority to the appropriate members. Set specific deadlines and live by them. Keep communication lines open and the information flowing in all directions. Write down everything and distribute copies so that everyone is on the same page and you avoid "I thought Joe was handling that."

Evaluation Meetings

Throughout the implementation of the plan, meetings should be held to monitor the progress of the effort. New challenges and opportunities will inevitably arise during this process, so a number of other meetings, such as problem solving or crisis management sessions, may be required. Periodic evaluation meetings see that the plan remains on time and on budget. I recommend an evaluation meeting at the conclusion of every project. How well did we do? Where did we foul up? How can we do this better next time? What did we learn? What, specifically, was our intent and did we achieve it? These meetings can be in-depth or mercifully brief depending upon your intent.

Marketing Meetings

Sometimes you have to sell an idea to your own organization so that you can sell your product or service to the public, such as when your marketing department presents the latest advertising, marketing or public relations campaign. These are called marketing meetings for obvious reason. They're important because if you can't sell your own team on your marketing concepts, they'll never be tried out there where they really count - in the marketplace.

Combination Meetings

Obviously there will be some overlap in meeting responsibilities. Other meetings will require that one type of meeting flows into another. For example, the situation with the potential new client (opportunity meeting) may require immediate action (decision meeting). The real key here is for the meeting leader to know when the group moves from one to the other, that the group has the same realization, and that everyone stays focused on the new goal.

Forarm With Formats

"A great leader is someone who can inspire and motivate average individuals to perform the work of extraordinary people."
Omar Periu

As a meeting leader you have a variety of meeting formats at your disposal. Which one you choose will depend on a number of factors including the purpose, goal, timeframe, participants, etc. Think about what you really need to accomplish and select the best one for the job. Here's a brief overview of your choices.

Guided Discussion

This is the format most of us know. A leader presents an agenda to a group of attendees who discuss the matter. The leader guides, but allows and encourages everyone to have input. Each item is handled one at a time and each item is either concluded or tabled before moving on to the next. Staff meetings and regular sales meetings are familiar examples.

Free For All

Everyone gets a say, in fact the leader should demand that everyone gets his or her say. Frequently, the leader will start with one person and then move around the table or room until each attendee has spoken. To prevent one person dominating the agenda, each person should be limited to a specific time frame, say three to five minutes. One real value of the free for all is that you can incorporate it within other formats. "Okay, I want everybody's opinion in sixty seconds or less. We'll start with Freda and work our way clockwise around the room."

Thinking On Your Feet

The goal here is to generate new ideas, to get your team to open up and really express its creativity. This is one session in which quantity is more important than quality. You want as many ideas as possible. Initially, every idea is as valuable as every other idea. You don't want to squelch your group's creativity at this stage. Later on you can weed out the impractical, impossible and hare-brained concepts.

It's important for the leader to encourage full and spontaneous participation. "No idea is too wild at this point, folks." Some managers have been known to bring toys to these meetings to free up structured minds and to get participants to "play" with ideas. Thinking on your feet sessions should be a lot of fun, but ultimately they should achieve serious results.

As with the free for all, you can often incorporate this format within other formats.

It's Just Me 'N You, Kid

One-on-one coaching meetings can be scheduled or they can be spontaneous. They can be very efficient because the number of attendees is so small and the personal time that can be invested in this type of meeting. The lack of other participants can also keep things less formal and more open. Still, a one-on-one meeting must have an intent, agenda and someone in charge to make sure things run efficiently. If you're the manager, allow the other person to bring his or her agenda to the meeting, also.

Even spontaneous meetings also need an agenda and a measure of control. "Got a minute, Bob?" can lead to a productive minute in the break room or a wasted afternoon listening to another bonehead idea from someone hiding from his or her responsibilities. Before you respond, determine the intent of the meeting and get an idea of how long that "minute" might last. If you're the one asking Bob, be sure to state why you want his time and how long you think you'll need his input.

Electronic Coaching Meetings

Sometimes all the participants can't be in one location at the same time. This is a particular challenge when a sales manager must communicate regularly with a sales team scattered over a large territory. With today's technology daily performance reviews are a must to keep people on track. And thanks to today's technology that's really no longer a challenge. The telephone, e-mail chat rooms, and video conferencing are now standard business practice. They allow managers to continue motivating a team one-on-one even when that team is in the field.

Hit And Run

Some meetings need to be swift, deliberate and highly focused - like a hit and run only it's no accident and the outcome is positive. The key for the leader is to make sure that the other person doesn't feel like you're intruding unnecessarily or that you are wasting time. If you conduct a hit and run meeting, be sure to keep it brief. Make sure that only those who are essential attend.

Again, you have a wide variety of meetings and meeting formats to help you and your organization make that move from "here" to "there." Which works best depends on many factors, but they all have one thing in common - a need for a plan. Let's go to Chapter Two and see how you go about creating great meetings by creating great plans.

THE ONE-MINUTE SUMMARY

- Focus on the intent of your meeting starting in the planning stages. Then stick with it.
- Virtually everyone today is involved in meetings. Study this book so that you can lead and speak well at time-effective meetings.
- Use your planning and leadership skills to overcome the chief problems with today's meetings including lack of leadership, lack of an agenda, dominating individuals, non-participating individuals, poor leadership, lack of preparation, timing problems, little or no focus, unrealistic expectations, distractions, no follow through, not sticking to the agenda, and meeting for no legitimate purpose.
- Decide what type of meeting you need. The main types are scheduled, opportunity/crisis, problem-solving, decision making, planning, implementation meetings, evaluations, and combinations of types. Your intent determines the nature of the meeting, so always be clear on your goals.
- Once the type of meeting is set, then focus on the most appropriate format: guided discussions, free for alls, thinking on your feet sessions, and one-on-one meetings.

Periu's Point

Winston Churchill said, "The price of greatness is responsibility." The price of conducting a great meeting is called leadership. Someone has to take the reins. If the designated leader abandons his or her responsibility, then someone else will fill that leadership gap. Chaos will rule and chaos is no way to run a successful and time effective meeting."

2

"The will to win is important, but the will to prepare is vital."

Joe Paterno

Develop A Meeting Plan

If the adage is true that a camel is a horse designed by committee, then clearly that committee acted without a clear intent or much of a plan. Poorly planned meetings are a drain on time, energy, enthusiasm, and group morale. They often cause more damage than they're worth. I know from valuable, and often painful, experience that every second invested in planning and organizing a meeting pays off in minutes and hours saved, efficiency and productivity, and in team spirit and motivation.

Do not make the mistake of believing you don't have time to plan a meeting or that you can successfully "wing it" without preparation. Invest the time now so you won't be wasting time and/or embarrassing yourself later. The first step is preparing the meeting agenda.

"Lucky breaks might occasionally knock on your door, but they'll never stay for dinner, dessert and coffee."

Omar Periu

Do You Really Need A Meeting?

This is the essential question. Few managers actually compute the real cost of a meeting. "Everyone's on salary, right, so what's the big deal?" Well, even for a minute it's a very big deal if those salaries are going to waste.

Here's a good way to evaluate the real cost of a meeting.

#1. Multiply every participant's hourly rate by the number of hours consumed during the meeting. You can estimate a salaried employee's hourly rate by dividing his or her salary (estimated if you don't know the actual figure) by a 40-hour week. This simple calculation will show you how quickly valuable employee time/expense mounts up.

#2. Figure in additional expenses such as travel, room cost (even if it's in your building), and even coffee and donuts. If someone must take a cab across town for the meeting, that cost is more than the cab fare. It must include that person's hourly rate as travel time.

You also have to figure in the cost to the organization. Here's that formula.

Divide the annual cost of each member's organizations' overhead by the number of working hours in a year.

Add all those numbers for the actual cost of the meeting. Those are hard numbers, but there's something else to consider and it's an important factor.

#3. Estimate the value to each attendee by not attending. In other words, what good to the organization could Bill, Kathy, Anthony and Dottie Mae accomplish if their time weren't taken up by an unnecessary meeting? If their time is better invested elsewhere, shouldn't they be...elsewhere?

> *"Without the management of time, you will soon have nothing left to manage."*
> William D. Reiff

> *Know where you're going in your speech, presentation, seminar or program. Even the briefest of meetings needs a well-prepared plan. Have a clear intent and a plan that includes a graceful exit strategy.*
> Omar Periu.

"Know where you're going in your speech, presentation, seminar or program. Even the briefest of meetings needs a well-prepared plan.

Have a clear intent and a plan that includes a graceful exit strategy."

Create An Agenda, Or You'll Create Chaos

The phrase "He's got an agenda" has taken on a negative aspect in recent years. It is generally used to mean the individual says one thing, but means something else. Okay, that happens all the time and in all facets of life. But when it comes to meetings, I hope and pray that you do have an agenda. Without a plan you really don't have a meeting. What you have is continuing chaos going nowhere.

An agenda is simply a statement, verbal or written, as to the intent of the meeting, how it will be handled, and the goal to be achieved. Essentially, it's the leader's playbook for the session. The agenda is not something to be taken lightly. As Coach Paterno said, it's vital.

Agendas appear in all kinds of formats. Some are pre-printed forms, others are memos, some are just words on a large notepad at the head of the table, and some are merely carefully planned thoughts in the mind of the leader. Regardless of format, your agenda should cover the following seven items.

#1. Time and Place. Never assume that everyone automatically knows where and when the meeting will be held. "We've always held it there" may mean nothing to the new member of the team or "old J.B.," the visiting VP from HQ. Try to avoid low energy times of the day, such as immediately after the lunch break. You want your team members at peak performance.

#2. Purpose. This item alone might kill a lot of unnecessary meetings. If you don't have an intent, a legitimate reason to hold a meeting, then please pass and allow everyone to get about the business of the organization.

#3. Title. A title isn't always necessary, but it does provide a sense of identity. A cleverly worded title can also bring a little fun, some pizzazz, or a sense of expectation to the agenda. For example,
Sales - Are We Slumping Or Jumping?
A Proposal For Boosting Sales During "Slow" Times.

The title should fit the tone of the upcoming meeting. Notice that the slightly humorous rhyme grabs the reader's attention, yet at the same time states a serious situation.

#4. Intent. Your managers, employees or team members cannot

reach the ultimate goal if they're marching down the road to different drummers. Again, the purpose of an agenda is to get from "here" to "there" efficiently and that means letting everyone know precisely where "there" can be found. That's intent.

#5. Length or estimated length of the meeting. If you don't provide some kind of parameters, conflicts are inevitable. You'll have people jumping ship throughout the meeting. If you have to make an estimate, state that it is an estimate and then do your best to respect the time and demands of your attendees by wrapping up as near to the closing time as possible.

#6. Attendees. List all of the people who will attend your meeting. Of course, if the meeting is with the entire fourth floor, you won't have to list each person. Keep in mind the rule of thumb that states the fewer the people the more effective the meeting. However many attend, the meeting should include everyone who needs to be there. If someone just can't make it and if you'd like his or her input, but a direct appearance isn't required, you can ask for a memo on the individual's opinion.

#7. Topics of discussion. I know there's a theory that secrecy equals control, but I don't buy it. Let everyone know the subject(s) of the meeting so everyone will be prepared.

Once you have your agenda, be sure to distribute it to the participants. Some leaders send out their agenda as a bulleted list while others prefer to use paragraphs in memo or letter form. The latter takes a lot of the structured formality out of the process. I prefer this low key approach, but choose the format that is best for you under the circumstances.

Try to keep your agenda short, sweet and hard to beat, to a page or less if possible.
Here's an example.
Sales - Are We Slumping Or Jumping?
A Proposal For Boosting Sales During "Slow" Times
November 12th, 9 a.m.
Conference Room #2
#1. (9:00)   Meeting Begins
#2. (9:10)   Reading of the minutes

#3. (9:15)   Discussion/Approval of the minutes
#4. (9:30)   Topic #1 - Consideration of the proposal on
boosting sales during "slow" sales periods.
#5. (10:30)   Voting on Topic #1
#6. (10:45)   RefreshmentsTry to keep your agenda short,
sweet and hard to beat, to a page or less if possible.
#7. (11:30)   Topic #3 - Report on New Product Tests Results,
the Benefits and Features, and Their Effect on Our New
Marketing Program
#8. (11:45)   Old/Other Business
#9. (11:55)   Topics for next meeting
#10. (12:00)   Meeting ends

I recently addressed an annual training conference. The evening before my presentation I covered all the details with the meeting planners, especially the need to distribute the agenda and workbooks prior to the speech because there were other speakers preceding me. The next day, as I started speaking, I noticed that neither the agenda nor the workbooks had been distributed. There were 1500 people in the audience, so the distribution took about 15 minutes and I had to "tap dance" by telling stories until everyone had his or her agenda and workbook. This unnecessary delay disrupted the entire flow of the day. It threw off the agenda, which upset the other speakers, and the audience had a lost of valuable time.

Periu's Point

If you plan on calling on a participant "cold," plan a brief introduction of that person. People caught short like that can panic. A valuable contribution could be lost due to that shock and fear. An introduction gives the called on person a moment to calm down and gather his or her thoughts. Here's something my mentors taught me - never ask a question to a member of the audience unless you know he or she will be able to answer the question.

Know Your Outcomes

In wrapping up this chapter I'd like to stress the importance of knowing your outcomes. That means doing everything possible to make sure your meeting accomplishes the goals you set for it. There are five major considerations.

#1. Be absolutely clear about the intent of your mission, and the intent of your meeting. Make sure everyone is not only on the same page, but in the same paragraph. Distribution of your agenda ahead of time is important, but don't neglect to mention the subject during the meeting. Of course, we all know your memos rival Shakespeare, but don't assume that everyone reads them with the same enthusiasm with which you write them.

#2. If you don't really need the meeting, then don't have it. This rule holds for regularly scheduled meetings, too. Again, "We've always had a meeting" is never a legitimate reason for holding one.

#3. Consider which elements will make your meeting a success and what elements will detract from accomplishing your goals. Incorporate the former and eliminate the latter. Do everything you can to enhance the productivity of the session.

#4. Think carefully of your attendees. Having upper level managers sit in may seem impressive, but their presence might also inhibit the free flow of conversation. Old Dub down in the maintenance department may seem out of place in the boardroom, but if you're evaluating maintenance procedures and costs, who is better qualified to give you an accurate view from the trenches?

#5. Choose your location carefully. Find the least intimidating, most open area you can. If possible alter the room to encourage the free flow of ideas. Open the curtains, turn off the piped in noise they call music, plan in refreshment breaks, and anything else that enhances the comfort of your participants.

THE ONE-MINUTE SUMMARY

- Invest the necessary time in planning your meeting. Such an investment is never wasted.
- Always ask if you really need to hold the meeting.
- Compute the hard costs of the meeting. One way to view meet ings is to follow the formula in this chapter. Note, if the mission can be accomplished by the meeting, the price may far outweigh the costs in the long run.
- Compute the benefits of not holding the meeting.
- An agenda should include: time, date, place, purpose, title, goal, estimated length, attendees, and topics of discussion.
- Every meeting must have an intent and agenda even if it's just in your head.
- Know your outcomes. Do everything possible to make sure the meeting will achieve its intent.

"It is not the going out of port, but the coming in, that determines the success of a voyage."
Henry Ward Beecher

"The mission of your meeting is the compass by which your ship will be guided through a successful voyage (meeting)."
Omar Periu

3

"The greatest revolution of our generation is the discovery that human beings, by changing the inner attitudes of their minds, can change the outer aspects of their lives."

William James

Before The Beginning -
Attitude Really Is Everything

Okay, you've just decided to make a speech, or have been asked to make a speech, or you have been told in no uncertain terms that you will make a speech. There are a lot of details to handle before you get to "A funny thing happened on the way to the podium." Your first concern is you and your attitude.

Wipe Out Your Baditude

Baditude is a good attitude gone bad and that can happen remark-ably fast when you realize you're soon to be standing in front of a group of folks listening to every pearl of wisdom dropping off your silver tongue...or every bonehead comment coming out of your yap. Whether the product is silver or yap really is up to you and the atti-tude you bring to the presentation.

The first professional speech I ever gave was for the Tom Hopkins International organization at the insistence of my mentor, Tom Murphy. I had only two weeks to work on that speech. Fortunately I was able to work with another mentor in the organization, Judy Slack, and I produced what I considered to be a good presentation.

The Friday before my Monday speech Tom looked it over and pro-nounced it dead on arrival. He gave me new bullet points and made me revise the entire speech. He really "got in my face," saying that I had not even come close to making my points. "We're not going to do this," he said.

That Monday I appeared before 400 people, including Tom, in Anaheim. You can imagine my fear. Unfortunately, the audience didn't have to use its imagination at all. I lost my confidence and my focus. I was so frazzled I couldn't even find the "on" switch for the overhead projector.

Every time I stepped up on a stage I thought about making my points. Today I still think about my points and my words, phrases, stories, pacing, my opening, middle and closing. I think about everything. Believe me, I understand fear of speaking. If you think you've got it bad at the next board meeting, think about addressing 400 people plus a highly-critical mentor.

Because I wanted to help others the way I had been helped, I made a total commitment to Tom Hopkins and Tom Murphy to see this thing through and make it work. Tom Murphy asked me to live in his home at six week intervals for more than a year so that he could help me on my delivery. Tom Hopkins helped me hone my speaking skills and develop an effective personal style.

The moral of this story is that you have to change your attitude. Regardless of what happens, where you speak, or who you speak to, you have to handle the situations as they come up. That truly horrible first speech could have ruined me if I had exhibited a "baditude." Instead, I worked hard to become a fearless speaker. And if I can do it, I know you can.

Begin immediately to think positive thoughts. Turn "I'm scared" into "Hey, I know this stuff...I can do this...the speech is a real boost to my career." Remember that the fear of public speaking is universal. People will respect and admire someone with the guts to take on the chore. Some of those folks could be a new client or the supervisor making your next job evaluation. Making a presentation is an excellent way to stand out from the crowd.

Anytime a negative thought wanders in, kill it. Kill it with malice aforethought. Do not allow it even a second for it to take root. Wipe it out. The challenge of public speaking is also an opportunity. Take

> *"Only passions, great passions, can elevate the soul to great things."*
> Diderot

full advantage of it. Develop enthusiasm and let that energy, excitement and passion for your subject show through. See yourself making a dynamic and well-received presentation. Make it mind accomplished long before you step up to that podium.

Program Your Program

You wouldn't create a superhighway, a rocket engine, or even a ball bearing without a production schedule. Use the same proven technique for creating your speech. Make a production schedule. Here's a format that I use. It works. Feel free to take it and adapt it to your needs.

Presentation Development Schedule

Date of Presentation:

_____

Topic Selected:

_____

Topic:

_____

Initial (rough) Outline:

_____

Complete Research:

_____

Complete Outline:

_____

Complete First Draft:

_____

Complete Final Draft:

_____

Visual/Other Aids Ready:

_____

Rehearsal Schedule:

_____

Developing and sticking to a schedule is important. It's way too easy to put off developing your speech until the last moment. After all, most people in the world dread public speaking. Lack of preparation will inevitably lead to a poor speech, a poor reception, and a self-fulfilled prophecy of failure. Start immediately. Develop a schedule. Stick to it. And then "blow 'em away" with your presentation.

Review Your Speech

A week prior to your presentation, go over your speech again and again and again. Check everything. Verify all your facts again. Make sure all your references are still up to date. Then make one final read-through to make sure everything is in proper form and that your speech actually says what you want it to say. Do you have a powerful opening that will immediately grab the audience's attention? Can you hold that attention for the first ninety seconds to three minutes? What's your "grabber" and does it really apply to your audience? Does your opening provide a base of understanding and lead into the middle of your presentation? Are you staying true to your intent throughout? Make sure you own it, that you don't even have to think about it once you step in front of your audience.

Is there an effective transition from the beginning to the middle? Will your audience know the topic of your speech by the time you make the transition?

Does the middle portion make a logical progression from one element to the other? Are those elements arranged in a logical order? Do they build toward your key point? Do you make your key point? By this time in your speech will you have made your case? What can be cut? What's missing?

Do you make an effective and seamless transition from the middle to the end? Are you providing your audience with signals that the end is approaching?

Does your ending completely and neatly wrap up your presentation? Are there any loose threads that will distract or disturb your audience? Is the wrap up fuzzy or fine tuned? Do your final words drive home your central message?

How effective is your "stinger?" Does your closing statement end with a bang or a whimper? Will your final few words carry the message home and, just as important, will your audience carry those words home? And last, but not least, will you achieve your intent for this meeting?

Rehearse For A Rewarding Experience

Sorry, perfect, even perfect practice doesn't make perfect. Nothing's ever perfect, but a lack of practice is a sure way to make an almost perfect fool of yourself. Rehearsal is essential, but don't overdo it. Four or five good run-throughs is generally enough to smooth out the rough edges. Rehearse in front of a friend or two who will provide you with honest feedback.

If at all possible, rehearse in the room in which you will make your presentation. Videotape technology is very affordable these days, so acquire or borrow a home unit and tape yourself making the presentation. Notice whether or not you voice those nagging "uhs...ahs...ers.." or any other nervous habits. I do this exercise at least once a month because bad habits can return or sneak in unnoticed.

Tom Murphy, bless him, used to charge me a dollar every time I said "you know" in a speech. I made this mistake so often that once I was fined $50 for one speech! You can use the same technique. Every time you make one of your common mistakes, have a friend or members of your family dock you a quarter.

I believe in visualizing your speech before you give it. Prior to every speech I make, I "experience" the entire thing. Mentally, I see, hear, feel, touch and smell everything that will occur. I see the people, feel the notes in my hand, and I hear the thunderous applause of an audience enjoying, receiving value, and getting inspiration from my words. I make the experience real before it happens. These, and

Shakespeare said, "He is well paid that is well satisfied." Then I'm exceptionally well paid. I love my work. I love speaking and the satisfaction I get from conducting successful meetings. I also love the fact that you'll soon share that feeling with me. Whatever your salary, commis-

> *sion or pay scale, when you take the principles in this book to heart and apply them, you will become well paid indeed.*
>
> Omar Periu

other exercises found in the appendix, will give you some familiarity with the arena of speaking at meetings and will significantly increase your comfort factor.

Last Minute Details For A First Rate Performance

Even if you've rehearsed in the meeting room, try to visit the area again before your actual presentation. Sometimes a speaker arrives by plane, is driven to the site, whisked into the room, and pointed to the podium with a hurried "You're on." If you're fortunate, you may have an opportunity to get in early and check out the facility.

Even the most basic speech is a complex procedure. A room that feels a bit brisk when empty can become sweltering when filled with human engines burning at 98.6 degrees. Is the temperature set right for the conditions of your presentation at the time of the presentation? The view of the city through the picture windows may be breathtaking, but will it take away from your presentation or will the light wash out your projected images? Where are your handouts? Is the cassette player in place? Will it play? Do you have back up tapes? Do you have extra projector bulbs? A lot of details go into making a great presentation. Any one of those details can foul it up.

A brief run-through of the facility can eliminate many of the potential pitfalls in your pathway. Here's a checklist of key areas.

Facility: Is the room reserved and for the right time and length of time? Are there enough chairs? Is the podium in place? Are the lights working? Is the temperature set properly for the time of the presentation? Are the sight lines good for the audience? Can you eliminate any last minute distractions?

Materials/AV Equipment: Are your projectors/playing equipment in place, hooked up, and ready to use? Is the flip chart set up and do you have a marker and spares? Where are your extra bulbs, batteries, and backups? Are the props in place? Does the microphone work? What about the extra microphone for questions from the audience?

Handouts: Do you have them and are they ready to be distributed? If you have multiple handouts, are they in order? Are there enough for all participants? Is someone assigned the task of handing them out? Are your sure?

Miscellaneous: Do you have adequate name cards, pens or pencils, notepads, give-aways, doohickies and thingamabobs, or whatever you need? Are there enough electrical outlets and are they live? Where are the: restrooms, telephones, smoking areas, fire escapes, etc?

Periu's Point

One of the greatest tips I can pass along is to arrive early and begin mingling. Meet and greet the audience, especially if it is small. I have even helped set up for the presentation. People just don't expect the speaker to help move tables, set up chairs, or pitch in on mundane tasks. They're delighted when it happens. You can build up a lot of good will and make a lot of friends with this simple act.

Refreshments: Are they in place or will they be delivered on time for the scheduled breaks? Will you get what you ordered and in the appropriate quantity?

Countdown!

Don't neglect yourself in those final moments before takeoff. If you start to feel those butterflies fluttering in your stomach, don't panic. Nervousness, under control, is a very good thing. It keeps us on our toes. Just take a few deep, slow breaths to calm yourself down. Concentrate your thoughts on the fact that you know your subject,

"Self-trust is the essence of heroism."
Emerson

you are well-rehearsed, and that this presentation is a very good move. Believe in yourself as much as I believe in you. You're poised on a moment of great opportunity. Seize it. Takeoff!

THE ONE-MINUTE SUMMARY

- Take care of the numerous and very important details between the time you finish writing your speech and making your presentation.
- Develop and maintain a positive attitude from start to finish.
- Erase all negative thoughts the moment they pop into your head. Immediately!
- Create a production schedule for developing your speech.
- Review your speech. Rehearse. If possible, rehearse in the room in which you will be speaking or at least get a good look at your speaking environment.
- Develop and use a last minute details checklist to avoid unpleasant last minute surprises.

4

"The man who complains about the way the ball bounces is likely the one who dropped it."

Lou Holtz

Managing Your Meeting

Public speaking is a skill, one that you can learn, master and continue to improve throughout your life. As your career path takes you further and higher you will soon discover a need for other skills. At some point you will be tasked with the job of managing a meeting. Don't shirk the duty. You can acquire and master that skill, too. Managing meetings presents you with the opportunity to showcase many of your skills and abilities. Remember, standing out in front of all of those people is an excellent way for you to "stand out from the crowd." That's how you grow and advance.

Why are so many meetings absolute failures? There are many reasons, but I believe the main fault is simply a lack of good management. The group leader makes a near-fatal mistake by losing control and then makes the decision completely fatal by failing to regain control.

So, how does a leader keep a meeting on track? Well, the first technique is the simplest, easiest, most basic and the least used.

Think Before You Speak

Or act. You can eliminate a significant number of problems before they ever arise by applying a little brain power. Think!

Have you distributed the agenda to all parties?

Is there enough time for all participants to study the agenda?

Have you studied the agenda and your supporting documentation?

Who are your allies?

Who will try to impose his or her personal agenda on the meeting?
What arguments are you likely to encounter?

Have you made contact with your allies to garner their support?

Notice that these concerns are basically political. Naturally, at the same time you'll be making sure the practical matters are also covered. Is the room reserved, the projector working, the coffee and donuts are ordered and so on.

> *"For success, attitude is equally as important as ability."*
> Harry F. Banks
>
> *I have met men and women with tremendous talent and ability who have failed to reach their potential as speakers and managers of time efficient meetings because of their "baditude." It's a killer - of morale, meetings and careers. Please don't become infected with the disease.*
> Omar Periu

Pacing, Racing Or Wasting Your Time

Pacing is critical to the success of any meeting. If the leader races along, people tend to drop off and get left behind. By the end of the meeting, few if any participants have a clear idea of what has just (literally) raced by. A meeting that drags has a similar effect. People realize their valuable time is being wasted. They resent the fact and either start daydreaming or working mentally on their own agendas. A good leader establishes a pace for the meeting, varying it if necessary according to the needs of that meeting, and then wraps on time with everyone feeling a genuine sense of accomplishment. There are four keys to good pacing:

- Start on time
- End on time
- Stick to your agenda so as to stick to your intent
- Schedule breaks

Start On Time

With very few exceptions, always start exactly when you have said you are going to start. An exception could be when your key speaker runs late. Even then, it might be possible to rearrange your agenda so that the speaker can participate and your meeting can still begin at the scheduled time. An adjusted agenda is preferable to a group of individuals thumping their collective fingers on the table.

If people arrive late, let them catch up on their own time. It is not the speaker's duty or the duty of the participants to bring a latecomer up to speed during the meeting. An exception might be made if the details of the meeting are so critical that it's worth reviewing them for the late shows. But backtracking is often frustrating for everyone else. Make sure it's necessary and not just misplaced courtesy.

Starting on time, as with arriving on time, is important to establish discipline, set up the proper flow or pacing for the meeting, and to show a little respect for the organization, the participants and the meeting itself.

End On Time

Ditto the previous sentence. Respect the time of your attendees and their other tasks for the day by bringing the meeting to a close at the time you have promised. There will be exceptions, of course, but a good leader will so effectively manage the meeting that these will be kept to a minimum. One of the main reasons so many speakers go over is that no one ever tells them their allotted time. Thinking they've got "all the time in the world," their ego takes over. A friend of mine was notorious for exceeding his allotted speaking time. The problem was solved when a good friend gave him a special birthday present. It was a big, smiling Buddha - with a big clock in its belly. My friend got the message and because it was presented in such a generous and fun way, everyone was all smiles, including his future audiences.

Remember that ending late automatically builds in a certain amount of resentment. You can't really help that. It's human nature. However, the leader who consistently runs over his or her meeting time will find that resentment building to a point where it interferes with achieving meeting goals. People will start looking for ways to duck those meetings, even those wonderfully brief one-minute meetings. People are creative. They'll find a way and there goes the agenda, which brings us to...

Stick To Your Agenda

A great leader never allows outside agendas to enter the conversation in the first place. "This isn't the time or place for that, Ralph." "We'll handle that in another meeting, Lilly." "That's not our topic today. Let's focus on the issue at hand." You can keep control without becoming a dictator. Be polite, but firm.

Schedule Breaks

Never allow a meeting to run more than 90 minutes without a break. One break per hour is a better and more efficient rule. Breaks are not lost time. They are investments in time in moving toward your ultimate goal. A break allows people to "get the blood circulating" to renew energy. They provide a moment of relaxation. They allow individuals a few moments to discuss issues one-on-one or in

Periu's Point

If you sense the meeting is beginning to drag, there are a number of techniques you can use to boost the energy: stand up, move around and speak at a slightly louder and/or faster pace; after getting full agreement from the other attendees, skip a couple of non-essential items on your agenda; ask for comment from one or more participants who are energetic speakers; reschedule items on the agenda that can be delayed to another meeting so you can still end on time.

private. They can be used by the leader to break the tension if the discussion gets a little heated.

Breaks are useful tools in the hands of a good leader. It's important to know how to read your audience. For example, I've learned that you can enhance your audience's experience by giving fewer breaks in the morning and more breaks in the afternoon. Everyone's fresher in the morning and can handle longer sessions. During the p.m. hour presentations, their energy starts to fade. This is especially true if you're addressing an annual conference in which everyone has been celebrating the night before.

I like to involve my audience. I often ask questions not only of individuals, but of the entire group.

"How many of you want to step up to the next level of achievement? Show me your hands!"

"How many of you believe in your product? Give me a 'Yea!'"

"Everybody say 'yes!' if you agree with me."

"Are there any winners here tonight? Hands up! Hands up! Hands up!"

"How many of you want to be better tomorrow than you are today?"

"Do you folks believe in yourselves? Then, repeat after me. I'm a winner! I'm a winner! I'm a winner!"

The idea is to get the blood flowing by getting their bodies moving. I'll have them stand up and do cheers or even moderate exercises. If the day is running a bit long and the audience is getting a bit restive, I've been known to toss inflated beach balls into the group - the bigger the audience, the bigger the beach balls. I try to get at least three or four balls bouncing in the air at one time.

Sometimes I'll step into the audience and get a couple of people to do a short roleplay to illustrate a point I've just made. The simple acts of raising hands, voicing an answer, or just playing around will often reenergize an entire audience which will have the same effect on the response to your presentation. Sometimes I'll split the audience down the middle and have one side challenge the other as to which will be the most enthusiastic throughout the day. As a prize, I'll offer members of the winning side a copy of one of my cassette tape programs. The point isn't the exercise, it's to get people moving, motivated, and to bring back their energy so everyone can get the most from the presentation.

Address Three Needs

A great meeting leader recognizes and accommodates the three basic needs inherent in every meeting:

- Needs of the agenda
- Needs of the group

- Needs of the individual.

The needs of the agenda should be obvious. You've drawn it up, distributed it to the participants, and everyone is on the same page, right? Not necessarily. Again, many people come to a meeting carrying baggage in the form of their own agenda. The leader's task is to make sure the real agenda is followed. State the intent of the meeting, get the group to agree with your statement, and then stick to it.

Group needs are people oriented rather than goal oriented. The group leader must foster and maintain an environment of teamwork. This doesn't have to be an us (committee) versus them (competitor, management, another committee, etc.) environment, just one that fosters united action toward a common goal. The group needs to feel that it is a...group. This is relatively easy to accomplish when the leader states the intent for the meeting, the goals, and the process.

Individual needs vary and you'll find a different list with every individual you ever meet. Robert Townsend, in Up The Organization, notes that humans are wanting animals; our behavior is determined by unsatisfied needs; and that these needs form an internal value hierarchy.

- Body - food, water, air, and the other essentials to preserving life.
- Safety - protection from the elements, etc.
- Social - a need to belong.
- Ego - a need for recognition from self and others.
- Development - we want to be better next day, month, year and the rest of our lives.

The last one is really important. Life is all about becoming. It's natural to desire daily personal growth. Growth, like diamonds, comes from intense pressure over time. I put myself under tremendous pressure to become the man I am today - a fearless speaker. And I keep that pressure up every time I prepare for and make a speech. As a CEO, an officer, manager or leader of any type, you must pressure yourself to become better on a daily basis.

The first three needs are pretty well covered in modern society. Most of us have a basic level of personal comfort, safety, and connections with society. Come on, everyone attending your meeting will be wearing good clothes, will have slept in decent housing, and will have been fed. The meeting leader then is concerned with only the latter two needs: ego and self-development.

This is a revelation of staggering proportions to the leader who will recognize and use this basic fact. You don't have to feed, clothe and shelter your participants. Recognize the achievements of people in your meeting and provide them with an environment for self-development. This isn't a New Age "touchy feely" proposition. It's a practical and proven way to motivate a group to achieving greatness.

Diagram of a Great Meeting

Activity

Meeting Begins _____

Good	Bad
Start on time	Late Start
	Late Arrivals

Intent of the Agenda _____

Group sticks with the intent	Group strays from intent
Discussions Orderly	Interruption of speakers
Polite	Rudeness
Conflict open and aboveboard	Backbiting, etc.
Everyone pays attention	

Small groups form/discuss issues _____

Arrive at a solution	
Forward Momentum	
Options explored	Infighting continues
Movement toward resolution	Movement toward chaos

Decision Point _____

Decision reached	Continuing argument
	No satisfactory resolution
	Animosity between participants

Meeting Ends _____

Recap major issues	No recap possible
Full agreement	Ineffective meetings grinds to a halt

In concluding this chapter, I'd like to note that there are only two types of leaders: those who manage and lead their teams and those that are managed and led by their teams. Which course you take is largely dependent upon the course you choose. Naturally, you will encounter "participants" who have other ideas. We'll see how to handle those folks in the next chapter.

> *"See everything, overlook a great deal,*
> *correct a little."*
> Pope John XXIII

THE ONE-MINUTE SUMMARY

- Think before you act, certainly long before you speak. Is what you are saying in line with your intent for the meeting?
- Plan every meeting, including the pacing of that meeting.
- Plan and use the four keys to pacing: start on time, end on time, stick to your agenda, and schedule breaks.
- Consider all of the needs of every meeting: needs of the agenda, the needs of the group, and the needs of the individuals participating. Cover all your bases.
- Individual needs are body, safety, social, ego and development.
- Ego and self-development are the two areas of concern to a meeting leader because the other physical needs have pretty well been taken care of in American business society.

5

"The easiest thing to be in the world is you. The most difficult thing to be is what other people want you to be. Don't let them put you in that position."

Leo Buscaglia

People Problems/People Opportunities

I believe it was Linus from the Peanuts cartoon strip who said, "I love mankind. It's people I can't stand." Whether or not you're a "people person," it still takes two to tango. You can't speak unless you have someone to speak to. Hmmm.... That's an audience and its size can range from a single individual to tens of thousands. Inevitably, the gathering together of people will create some challenges. How you handle those people and those challenges can have a significant impact on the success (or lack of it) of your meeting.

Periu's Point
You can handle any challenge if you don't lose your composure. Stay cool and you'll stay on top of the situation.

Consider yourself as the conductor of an orchestra. It's your duty to make sure everyone follows the score and plays in harmony. Any discordant sounds are most likely to develop from three specific areas:

- Late arrivals
- Participants who dominate the meeting
- Participants who do not participate

37

"People generally have two very good reasons for doing something: the reason they talk about and the reason they keep to themselves."

Omar Periu

Late Arrivals

Call the late arrival on his or her bad behavior. Note that such behavior is not acceptable, politely-yet-firmly, of course. And let that person catch up on his or her own time. Unless there is an extremely important extenuating circumstance, always start your meeting on time.

Dominating Personalities

Every group always has a leader. If the official leader doesn't lead, an informal leader will step forward and take charge. Remember that. If you do not lead, someone else will take over. It's likely that you, your intent and your agenda will soon be playing second fiddle under someone else's direction.

Dominating persons usually act from one of two motivations. The first is simply to dominate. This individual may have a deep need to be in control. He (or she) might also be under the impression that he has all the answers. Even if that's true, this person isn't the leader and does not have the right to take over that position.

The other personality is more concerned with destroying the effectiveness of the meeting than in making a positive contribution. I have an associate who was asked to make a presentation about his profession to a small group. One of the members claimed to have had a "horrid" experience with someone else in the same profession. She continually interrupted the speaker, contradicting his claims, and generally discounted every statement he made. In addition to speaking, my associate had been asked to provide a demonstration, but the woman's continuing interruptions were destroying his entire presentation. Finally, he spoke. "Ma'am, I admit that you are the exception to the rule. I believe your experiences are genuine, but you are the only one I've ever encountered or heard of who has had that experience. Now, these people are here to learn about and experience the other side of the story. We need to allow them that privilege."

The woman agreed and then left the meeting in a huff. The others in the group enjoyed the rest of a successful presentation and made a point of saying so.

A third personality type is the chatterbox. Again, it takes two to tango, so there's always a partner, even if it is a silent partner. The chatterbox jabbers away during your presentation, distracting at least one participant directly and usually several others indirectly. Nip this in the bud. Try direct eye contact. Think of all those close ups of Clint Eastwood in those spaghetti westerns. If that doesn't work, speak up.

Wait until the speaker's silence is noticed by those making the disturbance and then ask "Shall we wait?"

Ask, "Would you be willing to hold your side conversation until after the meeting?"

Ask, "Would you care to share your thoughts/ideas with the group?"

Ask, "Would you please join us as we continue?"

You can't allow a dominating personality to dominate your meeting. As a meeting leader you must assume and maintain control. Usually you can do so politely, even if firmness is required. Note that in the previous example, my associate agreed with his heckler and then addressed the situation. He was firm, yet polite and was able to continue the meeting. Note that he never directly attacked or accused his accuser. He addressed the inappropriate behavior, not the individual. That's an important technique. Remember it.

Periu's Point

Clashes within your group are healthy provided they are open, do not pull the group from the agenda, do not fall into name calling or personality baiting, and provided the leader remains in control. Defuse a tense situation by asking a neutral party to summarize each side or by asking someone a question that requires a factual (non-emotional) answer.

"Don't wrestle with pigs:
You get dirty and they enjoy it."
Anonymous

I was speaking at an event in which the audience of 2000 was all around me, something like theater in the round. About 45 minutes into my presentation I noticed that one of the attendees in the front rows was continually in motion. He moved from place to place to place, always positioning himself literally "in my face." You can imagine how distracting that can be. Everyone else was sitting politely in their seats, but this guy was constantly on the move.

I sought him out during the break, introduced myself and inquired about his conduct and asked if there was something I could do to help him stay in his chair and still get the full message. He replied that he was deaf and was merely trying to be in a position to read my lips. His actions were actually quite flattering. I asked him to remain seated and during the rest of my presentation I moved my body toward different parts of the audience, but I kept my movements so minimal that he didn't miss a word. He was able to read my lips without disturbing the rest of the attendees. The point is simply that I kept my cool. That allowed me to solve my problem with a disturbance in the audience while at the same time enhancing the presentation for the deaf gentleman (and the rest of the audience, too.)

Another example of keeping your cool happened during a speech in Tulsa. The temperature was very hot and a woman passed out. I asked for people to rush to her aid. When it became obvious that she couldn't be moved, I didn't panic. I merely called a break, asking all the attendees to network among themselves. After the paramedics took the woman out, I continued the presentation and still received an ovation. Keep your cool. Keep your audience. And stick with your intent and agenda.

The Nonparticipating Participant

Sometimes the conductor has to drag a good performance from a player. Every once in a while, you'll encounter an attendee who is "shy" simply because he or she is unprepared. Most often, however, that shyness is genuine. Remember, most people fear public speaking more than death itself. You have to find a way to draw out these people and make them productive members of the team. That's part of being a leader.

One way is to make a point of calling on them to speak during the meeting. Plan this carefully so that you pick a subject the individuals know well and will be confident handling. A poor topic selection could set back or ruin your plans to bring this person out. It's okay to let someone know in advance you'll be calling. "Say, Billie, I'd like you to speak a moment on the XYZ project in next Tuesday's meeting." That's all it takes. Billie will be prepared, will speak well, and will have her confidence enhanced. Again, you're a team leader. It is your responsibility to make sure everyone on the team contributes to the team effort.

THE ONE-MINUTE SUMMARY

- Working with people means working with some problem people. Evaluate your attendees and prepare for whatever blocks they might throw your way.
- Problems will most often occur in three key areas: late arrivals, participants who dominate the meeting, and participants who do not participate. Have a plan in mind to handle any of these problems.
- A leader of time effective meetings maintains control of his or her environment.
- See that everyone in the committee has an opportunity to voice his or her opinion or to make a statement. Be prepared to encourage shy members to speak and to control anyone who tries to take over. Again, think these problems through before the meeting.
- For involvement call on everyone, even if you have to prepare shy members in advance.

6

"The riddle does not exist. If a question can be put at all, then it can also be answered."

Ludwig Wittgenstein

Prepare For Questions

You will have to handle questions. Even if you do not have an official Q&A session, even if you announce that you will not be taking questions, even if you make a mad dash for the back door the second you close your presentation, someone will raise his or her hand. At that point you have to deal with the situation. The fear of answering questions is just another element of the fear of public speaking. It's something you have to overcome and the best way is to just get in there and start providing the answers.

I know one speaker who actually turned most of his presentations into Q&A sessions. He had an outline of where he was going, but he knew his subject so well that he allowed the audience to pretty much dictate the direction and flow of his presentation. I don't recommend that approach for most presentations, but it certainly is a unique way to handle the problem of questions.

I can't tell you the answers to all the questions that will be flying your way, but let me share with you how to handle different types of questions.

Lawyers are warned to never ask a question without first knowing what the witness will say. Speakers don't always have that luxury, but should know their material so well that they're not often thrown by tough questions.

Omar Periu

43

Have No Fear, Questions Are Near

Never fear or resent questions. Welcome them for two very basic reasons:

1. Questions provide you with an opportunity to continue achieving your intent.
2. Questions mean people are listening to what you are saying. They want more.

Question Yourself

By that I don't mean doubt yourself. I mean ask yourself questions that can (and probably will) be generated by your speech. Mentally put yourself in the audience. Think of yourself as a friendly participant and see what questions arise. Then play devil's advocate and become a hostile critic. If someone attacks your position, what are the likely arguments and/or questions? Be honest with yourself and don't hold back. Try to anticipate every possible question and then come up with honest, believable and understandable answers.

I recommend that you write down these answers. I don't want you to bring those notes along as crib sheets, though. Forget that. You need to appear spontaneous. Writing down the answers will help imprint those answers on your brain so you won't need notes. You'll more easily bring up the information and be able to put it into the exact context of the specific question.

Don't be afraid to go a little "whacko" in developing a list of questions. As you'll soon discover, a portion of many audiences is comprised of people who ask some really strange questions. Hey, whackos deserve answers, too. Be prepared.

> *"'Why' and 'How' are words so important that they cannot be used too often."*
> Napoleon Bonaparte

> *"During your Q&A sessions you'll also get to meet their cousins Who, What, Where and When."*
> Omar Periu

Count Your Questions

This is just a rule of thumb, but if you have more than about 20 questions stemming from your presentation (20 minutes or so duration), then you've probably left a few holes in your speech. You'll need to address some of them while you can. Remember, you're not trying to discourage questions, but you don't want to backtrack and cover areas you should have already addressed.

Practice Your Answers

That's right. Practice answering questions. If you can, have a friend feed you the questions you've come up with on your own - pro and con, easy and hard. You might want to put a little more emphasis on the harder questions, but don't pass on the easy ones. Many a speaker has been tripped up on a so-called easy question or the even tougher follow-up question it set up. Get honest feedback on how you handle those questions. Are your answers truly honest? Did you really answer the question asked or did you dodge the issue? If your goal is to dodge an issue for the moment, how well did you do? Did your answers appear genuine? If you can't rehearse in front of an audience, practice with an audio recorder or, even better, film yourself. Play back the answers and evaluate your responses as if you were an attentive member of the audience. Practice several more times just to make sure your answers seem natural. Listen particularly for "uh...ah...er..." and so on. Such pauses make you appear nervous, unsure of yourself, or even that you're hiding something. An honest speech delivered in a manner that suggests a lack of honesty will make a negative impression on the audience.

> *"Questions are never indiscreet, answers sometimes are."*
> Oscar Wilde

You're A Speaker, Not A Tap Dancer

Some questions just don't apply to the subject at hand or will not advance the intent of your presentation. It's okay to avoid the situation to stay on track. Simply say, "If you will see me during the break, I'll be happy to answer all your questions."

I have an associate who often speaks on political subjects to different audiences. He announces at the beginning of his presentation that some of the answers will be "I don't know." He also makes an offer to serious researchers, that if he does not provide an answer in the presentation, he will be available after the presentation to provide direction for further research. He's so convinced of the rightness of his cause that he invites skeptics to do their own research to prove him wrong. "I'll help," he says. Honest answers are always the best answers even if you and the questioner aren't 100 percent satisfied with that answer.

A good speaker should develop the skill of thinking on his or her feet. For example, Dr. Ken McFarland tells of a famous surgeon who was asked to tour the country speaking on a special technique, but he was afraid of flying. Not wanting to lose the opportunity, he bought a big limo, hired a chauffeur and began the tour. He and the chauffeur eventually became good friends along the way. One evening the doctor was pontificating a bit, saying that his technique was so technical that no one else in the world could make his presentation. His chauffeur laughed. He said that after a year and a half on the road listening to the presentation, he could give the same speech word for word. "In fact, I could give it better than you," he said. The doctor disagreed and offered a wager. They would switch places at the next speech on the tour. The next evening the doctor dressed as the chauffeur and stood at the back of the room while the chauffeur gave the speech. Much to the doctor's embarrassment, his employee delivered an excellent speech. He even got a standing ovation. At the end of the presentation, the host noted that there was some extra time available. "Would you mind taking a few questions, doctor?" What was the "doctor" to do? He agreed and prepared for the worst. The first member of the audience to raise his hand asked a very technical question. The chauffeur hadn't a clue as to the answer.

"Are you a doctor?" he asked.

"Yes," was the reply.

"Well, sir, I am amazed. The answer to that question is simple. In fact it's so simple, I will allow my chauffeur in the back of the room to answer it for you." The point of the story is to never let questions throw you. They are merely opportunities to advance your point of view. Don't panic. Think. And then speak.

Make Notes, Take Notes, Never Forsake Notes

It's much better to have a few words or sentences on hand so you can phrase your response in any manner, any length or any terminology you desire - on the spot. Again, spontaneity is one of your best assets.

> *"The smart ones ask when they don't know. And, sometimes, when they do."*
>
> Malcolm Forbes

It's Okay To Say "I Don't Know."

You will never impress anyone (for long) by trying to tap dance around an issue. That's one of the reasons the phrase "no comment" was invented. If you don't know, it's far better to admit it than to attempt a doomed effort at obscuring your lack of knowledge.

Please understand that people recognize speakers as people, individuals with all the frailties, faults and foibles that come with the territory of being a human being. They're an amazingly forgiving lot, provided you're honest. Lincoln was right. You can't fool all of the people all of the time, so why make the effort? If the answer is important, you can always promise to find it and get back to the individual at a later time.

Remember the old adage, honesty is the best policy, even if it makes you uncomfortable for a brief moment. Respect your audience and they'll return the favor.

Periu's Point

You don't have to be rude to control an audience, even when things come up you'd rather not discuss. For example, let's say you don't want to answer questions at the moment, yet someone raises his or her hand. My mentors taught me to simply look the other way and state that I'll be answering all questions during the Q&A session at the end of the program, or that I'll be available during the breaks. This technique allows you to avoid unwanted questions without hurting the feelings or embarrassing the person with the raised hand.

THE ONE-MINUTE SUMMARY

- Know your subject matter inside and out. Every presentation will generate questions.
- Anticipate questions and practice your answers. Rehearse the answers and the confidence and style in which you give them.
- Embrace questions. They provide you with an opportunity to continue making your point and achieve the intent of your presentation.
- Keep a positive attitude about questions. They mean people are listening to what you are saying. They want more. Be sure to give it to them.
- Never try to fool an audience.

Part II.

Becoming
A Fearless
Speaker

7

"Remember, every time you open your mouth to talk, your mind walks out and parades up and down the words."

Edwin H. Stuart

Analyze Yourself

I reviewed hundreds of books and films on speaking as "thought starters" for this book, and I noticed that nearly every one had a section on "knowing your audience." That's an important subject, and I'll be covering it in the next chapter. Before you analyze your audience and the needs of that audience, there's another need-to-know and that's to know yourself. Shakespeare's Polonius said, "This above all, to thine own self be true and it must follow as the night the day thou canst be false to any man." If you first know yourself and are true to yourself, then you cannot be false to your audience.

A fearless speaker adapts his or her words and phrases, body language, stories and style to meet the needs of each audience. Knowledge of self is necessary to make those kinds of adaptations to connect with each audience.

Your mission might require you to carry an identical message about finance to a board of directors, a group of third world investment bankers, or the local retired ladies' investment club. Adapt your presentation to the language of the audience so that you will be easily and completely understood. For example, let's say you believe that if your advice isn't followed, complete and utter financial ruin will follow. Speaking to an Ivy League crowd of CEOs, you might make reference to "floating down the Acheron" if they don't follow your

51

advice. The Acheron is the ancient mythical river flowing through hell, in this example a financial hell. When carrying the same message to a group of blue collar investors you might say, "If you don't, as all farmers know, 'it'll be too hot to plant.'" And the ladies investment club might hear you say, "If you don't do this, you can expect nothing short of 'heck' on earth." The point has nothing to do with intelligence and everything to do with the language and experiences of the audience.

How can you possibly know how to adapt your presentation to different audiences if you don't know yourself? You can't, so how do we go about discovering...you?

> *"Men who know themselves are no longer fools; they stand on the threshold of the Door of Wisdom."*
> Havelock Ellis

> *"Knowing yourself is the first and essential step in knowing all that you need to know."*
> Omar Periu

Your Personality Is One Of Four Basic Types

Everybody on the planet is one of four basic behavioral types:

#1. *Mainspring* - task oriented, perfectionist, wants the facts and figures.

#2. *Scholar* - direct, controlling and dominant, thinks on his/her feet, self-contained.

#3. *Buddy* - supportive, loyal, sensitive and attentive. Relationships are key.

#4. *Spokesperson* - interactive, friendly, good conversationalist, spontaneous, intuitive.

Different texts have different names for these types. Some call them the "director," the "thinker," the "socializer," or the "relater." Regardless of the title, the meanings are the same. Naturally, there is overlap and you will find varying degrees of personality shading, but essentially each of us fits rather neatly into one of these categories.

To "know thyself" in our present context means knowing your personality as it relates to each audience you address. What do you want to say? Where is your passion? What do you want the audience to hear and understand? How can you hit them in the heart? What do you want the audience to take with them after your presentation? How well you achieve your goals depends upon how well you relate to your audience. How well you relate depends upon knowing which trait is dominant. Only by knowing yourself can you adapt yourself to the varying needs of different audiences.

For example, the "little old ladies" in the investment club may be typical grannies baking cookies for the kids, knitting and purling in a rocker on the front porch, and saying things such as "isn't that sweet" when a grandchild brings her a handful of wild flowers. Once she gets in that investment group, she may put on the green eyeshades, take out her palm pilot calculator, and become as sharp a business person as you'll ever meet. Your presentation will need to use the language of facts and figures and not cookies and milk. If you're a Spokesperson type, you will have to adjust your presentation, your style and your examples to fit the needs of that Mainspring audience. You can't do that unless you know your own personality. Let's take a quick look at those personality types. Keep in mind that one personality is no better or no worse than the others, just different. It's useless and even counterproductive for a Buddy to want to be a Mainspring or a Spokesman to want to be a Scholar. We are what we are and thank God for it. Know the real you and make the absolute best of the material you've been given to work with.

Periu's Point

Self-praise, held in control, is a good and necessary process. We are often our most vocal and deadliest critic. It's good to remind ourselves that we're good people, we're making contributions to society, and that we're on a road to real achievement. More important than self-praise, however, is honest self-appraisal. Know thyself.

The Mainspring Drives The Process

Mainsprings have a "driving need" to be in charge of any situation. They're action oriented people who chafe at idleness. They just have to be moving toward some goal. Their actions are usually quick and decisive and based upon logical thinking and evaluation of the facts. Acts that may on the surface appear impetuous, may actually be based on long hours of contemplation. They are good managers who do not shy away from conflict and in fact may see controlled conflict as a positive way of getting feedback. They see and focus their attention on the big picture and prefer to delegate details to others. Like television's Detective Joe Friday of Dragnet, they want "just the facts, ma'am." Mainsprings are independent, competitive and cool in a crisis. They aren't really interested in "touchy-feely" approaches to problems and will, whenever possible, act on their own. If you are a Mainspring, you probably need to balance your drives by listening more, work on your lack of patience, be a bit more sensitive to the needs of others, take the time to explain your actions when appropriate (more often than you think), and for goodness' sake, relax.

Sitting At The Scholar's Station

That's an apt description of the Scholar personality's office, a station where information is accepted, examined in detail, filed appropriately and at the right time acted upon. The Scholar is also a logical thinker, but is much slower to act than the more aggressive Mainspring. The term "paralysis by analysis" was coined for these people. They have an overriding need to be right, and therefore have a need for lots of data and lots of time to study that data. They are cautious loners, often intellectuals, who prefer to avoid conflict. They like to be recognized for the accuracy of their data and conclusions. If you ask them for the time of day, they might launch into a lecture on how to build a watch.

To work better with others, the Scholar should try to be a little more flexible and accept the fact that change is inevitable and often a good thing. He or she should make efforts toward making decisions more rapidly when possible. Scholars need open interaction with co-workers. Loosen up. You'll get to know a great group of people.

> *"He who knows others is clever, but he who knows himself is enlightened."*
> Lao-Tzu

Social Consciousness

The Buddy personality is a social creature who has a need for communication with other people. These folks are often the "life of the party" who can act spontaneously and move quickly and easily from one goal to another. They can see the big picture, but are bored with the day-to-day details necessary to achieve it. They are usually big dreamers with the ability to charm others into following that dream - even if they jump ship later to move on to another dream. Buddy personalities need to receive positive feedback and praise from superiors and coworkers.

Buddy personalities are rather unorganized and need to focus more on organizational skills and less on their emotions. They should take a lesson from the Scholar personality and invest more time in research and fact-finding. They should work on finishing the task at hand before leaping toward the next day dream.

Spokespersons

If you have good "people skills," like to work with others without conflict, and if you put a premium on tranquility, then you're a Spokesperson. These folks are logical thinkers who seek security in facts and figures, but they are the most personable of all four types. They like people and are your typical team players. They are good listeners and are very supportive. They like to get to know others, build strong relationships and are concerned about how any action will affect the cohesion and effectiveness of the group. Spokesperson personalities can be overly sensitive, which makes it easier for other types to assert themselves and even achieve dominance over them. Spokespersons should realize that it's perfectly okay to say "no" to a bad idea. Open disagreement, even controlled conflict, will not destroy the group and may even make it stronger.

Which personality type fits you best?

Take some time to analyze yourself. What makes you you? Once you know and understand yourself, you are ready for the next step in becoming a fearless speaker. You're ready to analyze your audience.

> *"Knowledge is power, if you know it about the right person."*
> Ethel Watts Mumford

That's a funny line, but it's true and especially if applied to yourself. Self-awareness is real power.

THE ONE-MINUTE SUMMARY

- Before you can accurately analyze an audience, you must invest the time to analyze and get to know yourself.
- You can't relate effectively to the needs of an audience and achieve your intent unless you first know yourself.
- The four basic personality types are: Mainspring, Buddy, Scholar and Spokesperson. It is important to understand the characteristics of each type, which one is your dominant trait, and how you can communicate effectively to the others.
- Everyone will fit into one of these personality types.

8

"*You must know your audience.*"

Ed Wohlmuth

Analyze Your Audience

Let's assume that you know your subject matter and, equally important, you now know yourself. You're a mainspring, a buddy, a scholar or a spokesperson. Now, what's the dominant personality of your audience?

A preacher advertised his small town revival for weeks in advance. Unfortunately, only one person showed up for the first night's sermon. The preacher asked if the attendee would just like to chat. "Heck, no, Parson. I drove two hours to hear you preach. I may only be one person, but I count, don't I? " He got his wish. The traveling preacher let fly with his most powerful sermon. He quoted the Old Testament. He quoted the New Testament. He told impassioned stories and after 90 minutes of pure "fire 'n brimstone," he closed with an extended solo of Shall We Gather At The River. After the close, he asked, "So, what do you think?" "Golly, Parson, I wanted a sermon, but 'ya didn't have to dump the whole thing on me!" he said.

The point to the story is to know your audience. As Jim Rohn says, you don't shoot a rabbit with a cannon. I mean, you can and you'll certainly bag your game, but there's not much of the rabbit left. A fearless speaker gives a speech that is the size of his or her audience. The bigger the audience the bigger you have to be. The smaller the audience, the more intimate you become. Again, always think of the needs of your audience.

How can you turn your personality strengths and weaknesses into positive means of expression to that audience? You have to know 'em to speak to 'em. I think it's very important to know the nature of your audience before you prepare your presentation. Again, even if you know the subject matter inside and out, you will use different tools and techniques to reach the personalities of different audiences.

> *"In order to speak short upon any subject,*
> *think long."*
>
> H.H. Brackenridge

Go To Market

Essentially, analyzing an audience is nothing more than market research. So, let's take a lead from marketing professionals and break down the makeup of your audience:

Age
Sex
Education
Occupation
Economic status
Religion
Ethnicity
Political Affiliation
Cultural background
Size
Knowledge of the subject of your speech

These are basic demographics, but they will give you a good, basic preview of your audience.

Age

Naturally, the members of your audience will vary in age - unless you're addressing the "Babies of 1984 Club" or some such group. It's important to know the age range of your audience. Is it predominantly retirees, middle-agers, or young people? The style of your presentation, your pacing, your use of humor or the lack of it, the stories you use as examples and other factors will be in large part dictated by the age of your audience. You can't effectively use a reference to the Beatles "I Wanna Hold Your Hand" to a group of young people who might be shocked to discover that Paul McCartney sang in another

58

group before Wings. A reference to the excesses of Ozzy Osbourne will probably be lost on an audience who still enjoys Glenn Miller and Benny Goodman.

If you're speaking to young audiences, be particularly wary of trying to be "hip." For example, by the time this book is in print chances are there'll be an entire new group of rock 'n rollers practicing excess behaviors. References to Ozzy Osbourne could mark you as a person trying too hard to be one of the group. You risk losing them before you really begin. Try saying "that's groovy and boss, man, I dig it" to one of today's spiked-haired young people and see what kind of reaction you get. If you must use the current lingo, be sure to check it out with someone who knows and speaks the "language."

Sex

A female audience may require you to use the word "she" in most of your examples. An all male audience would probably respond better to "he" in your stories and an equally mixed audience might respond better to "he or she." Keep in mind you can overdo the political correctness thing. "He and/or she enters his and/or her workstation and, using his and/or her key, engages his and/or her machine to begin his and/or her work so that he and/or she may complete a satisfactory production run during his and/or her shift." See what I mean?

Education

I believe with Will Rogers that we're all equally ignorant in some areas. The complement to that is that we're all equally smart in some areas. We're all intelligent beings and although there are a few exceptions, those exceptions cross all educational lines. There's many a college graduate who could be legitimately addressed, "'Ya dummy!" And there are many unschooled persons who have a vast store of wisdom and experience. The point is to tailor your speech to the educational level of each specific audience.

It is a foolish speaker who addresses a blue collar audience as if they were kindergarten students. "Now, what this means (for you simple folks) is..." Talking down to any audience is a sure way to shoot yourself in the foot.

The rule works both ways. In business today, particularly in manufacturing, management has realized the value of listening to the advice of people out there on the line, the folks who work in the trenches. (This obviously applies also to salespeople on the road, people who deal directly with the public, and folks in numerous other areas.) It's not unusual at all for a blue-collar production manager to address a management or technical team of university graduates on some area of personal expertise. That manager has to take into consideration the knowledge level of the audience on the specific subject at hand. The group may have an extensive knowledge of production theory, but when the speaker says, "Since our PEL limits can't exceed fifty micrograms of lead per cubic meter of air averaged over an eight-hour day, we require action at 30 micrograms per cubic meter of air, time weighted averaged, based on an eight-hour work day," the words may be "Greek" to the assembled group. What is the knowledge base of your audience?

Occupation

If for no other reason than to tailor your stories to the audience, it's necessary to know their occupational status. Are they all managers? Do they all manage the same type of organizational structure? Do they manage the same type of facility? Are they CEOs, vice presidents, sales managers, department managers, self-employed plumbers, or a group of new hires. If they're upper level managers, do they manage an automobile dealership, a manufacturing plant, a financial institution or a government think tank? What they do for a living will affect how you say what you say to them.

Economic status

Again, your approach and sometimes the focus of your presentation will vary according to the needs of the audience. Let's say that you're speaking about financial investments. A crowd of entry level managers will most likely be more interested in growth so that they can build a base for the future. You might recommend an aggressive investment policy. An audience of well-off retired corporate presidents will be more interested in protecting their existing financial base, so your advice might be more conservative.

Religion

Be sensitive about the way you bring your faith into your presentation. Politics and religion are hot button issues and the wrong word in the wrong place can lose an audience or even turn it hostile. Today's society is full of people just waiting to be "insulted" so they can react wit pent up indignation. At the same time you should remember that 94% of the people in America believe there is a God, and you risk offending them when you don't include God in your presentation. You'll notice references to God in virtually all of my works. I am saying to be aware of the sensibilities of others and show respect and courtesy toward all beliefs.

Ethnicity

The same rule applies here. You get the point.

Political Affiliation

Ditto. Politics affects every area of our lives and should be at least considered when making a presentation. Popping off with your personal take on politics may boost your ego, but it may also bust your presentation. Unless the subject of your presentation is political, avoid overly promoting your favorite political party, politician or cause.

Cultural background

One of the great strengths of America is the constant infusion of new blood, new ideas, and new cultures. This powerful and delightful mix requires a bit of careful thinking on the part of America's fearless speakers. For one thing, you don't want to accidentally offend someone coming from another culture, either as a U.S. citizen or as a visitor. For example, in some countries, it's considered impolite to shake hands. A bow is more appropriate. In some nations the simple act of handing over a business card is almost a ritual.

I'm not saying you have to go overboard on cultural sensitivity. You can't please all the people all the time. But I am saying that you should be aware of other cultures and how that background could and should affect your presentation.

Size

In a practical sense, the size of your audience will dictate numerous factors in your presentation. A small group may allow you to be intimate and even one-on-one with some of the members. You can engage in an interactive performance. A large crowd may require a microphone, a stage, a lectern and large-format visual aids. Generally, you can be more familiar and intimate in a smaller group.

As I mentioned earlier, be as big as your audience. Large crowds are obviously more difficult to control. You have to expand your presentation and yourself to fit the expanded size of the crowd. If your audience is an elephant instead of a rabbit, that cannon might come in real handy. You'll need more humor or more drama, more excitement, more emotion and more "umph!"

> *"A business man's judgment is no better than his information."*
> Robert P. Lamont

> *"The more informed you are about your audience, the better your presentation and the more satisfied your audience."*
> Omar Periu

Knowledge of your subject

A friend of mine, an advertising copywriter, says one of the biggest mistakes made in his industry is the assumption that the buyer knows as much about the product or service as his client, the seller. This misconception leads to all kinds of miscommunication. Words, phrases and expressions that are commonly understood "in the biz" are meaningless to the consumer and, therefore, go unrecognized. And the product or service goes un-bought.

Never underestimate your audience or their level of knowledge about your subject, but do not assume they are as up to speed as you. If they are, great, but verify before you start.

In the end, remember that regardless of how great a fearless speaker you may be, you're nothing without an audience. Like the actor who "struts and frets his hour upon the stage," we speakers need someone to speak to. Analyzing your audience is a great way to make certain your speech deserves more strutting than fretting.

Preparing a good speech in many ways involves what Tony Jeary, in <u>Inspire Any Audience</u>, calls a "funneling process." Information is fed in at the wide end at the top. It flows through a number of steps before emerging at the narrow end. In other words, the process refines your presentation. These steps are as follows.

1. **Define the desired results.** "What do I want my audience to take home with them after I make my speech?" What is your intent?
2. **Know your audience.**
3. **Remember the three needs:** your own, your audience's needs, and the needs of the individual.
4. **Keep your presentation focused** on a small number of clearly defined goals, each enhancing the achievement of your intent.
5. **Examine your presentation from the point of view of your audience.** When the information finally emerges, you have defined the core objectives of your speech.

THE ONE-MINUTE SUMMARY

- Study your audience in advance. You must understand them as much as possible so that you can relate and make an effective presentation.
- Use a market research approach to defining your audience. Analyze the data.
- Consider your audience's age, sex, education, economic status, religion, ethnicity, political affiliation, cultural background, size, and knowledge of the subject of your speech. Include the audience's dominant "personality" in your plans.
- Use the Event Questionnaire in this book to help analyze your audience.

9

"An architect's arch is a heap of stones until and unless it is organized and grouped around a keystone. The keystone holds the pattern together. So it is with life. Unless there is some keystone conviction by which experience is organized, the individual remains little more than a bundle of feelings. "

Martin H. Scharlemann

Outline Your Presentation

I heard a great story in church when I was a kid. Our teacher, making a point about preparing a spiritual life, told us of a highway construction company project. The company wanted to pave roads all over the county so more people could get from here to there. They loaded up the concrete trucks and began pouring roads throughout the county. Unfortunately, in their hurry to get as many roads built as possible, they neglected to set up concrete forms to hold the material in place until it set. The concrete just flowed left and right over the hills and valleys, always following the path of least resistance. After all their work, the company was left with an uneven, unsightly, unusable concrete mess.

The lesson applies to meetings and speaking, too. If you make the attempt without first building a structure, you'll have nothing more

65

than a big mess on your hands or, rather, on your lips. The structure of a great speech is called the outline.

> *"There is nothing wrong with having nothing to say - unless you insist on saying it.*
> Anonymous
>
> *"When you do have something to say, it's vital that you say it with passion, enthusiasm, and a clear intent. If you don't have something to say, then please don't."*
> Omar Periu

The Keystone Is Key

An associate of mine who is a professional writer says one of the worst errors a writer can make is to just start writing without a purpose and a plan. The plan is the outline and the purpose is the keystone. As in the above-mentioned quote, the keystone is the central building block that holds together the entire presentation.

What is your keystone? What do you really want to say? What message connects and holds together your entire presentation? What is your true intent? In the words of all those cereal company contests, you should be able to state your keystone (intent) "in 25 words or less."

- My purpose (mission) is to convince the board of directors to approve the purchase of the ABC Company assets.
- My purpose is to inspire the sales team to achieve our increased sales goals.
- My goal is to convince my company president of the practicality, desirability and financial wisdom of moving our East Coast manufacturing facility closer to our distribution center in the Midwest.

Your purpose should be easily and quickly stated, easily understood by all (especially you), and measurable. It's a goal, plain and simple. With that single, overriding purpose in mind, you can begin assembling your presentation outline.

Format Doesn't Matter

I like to use the Roman numeral/letter system most of us learned in grade school. I find it easy to use, fast, and a great aid in logical organization.

I. Introduction
- A. Greeting to audience
  1. Thank host
  2. Recognize John Doe
  3. Overview of your presentation. State what you are going to cover.
- B. Humorous story
  1. I get stuck in elevator story
  2. Bridge to getting stuck in our careers

II. Plan Your Career Early
- A. It's never too soon to begin
- B. Compile information
- C. Research
- D. Summary

If you don't like that format use another, anything that provides a level of confidence and comfort. I once saw a photograph of President Eisenhower taken just before he made a public address. He held a large note card in his left hand. The photographer was behind the president so the notes on the president's card were easily visible. His outline was nothing more than a stacked series of single words. That's all the outline Ike needed.

Another format is to use a lot of note cards, each one representing a point, an example or a story. You can rehearse by moving the cards around a table, organizing and reorganizing them according to the best flow for your speech. Once you have the order in mind, print the number on the cards. A gust of wind or a slip of the hand can scatter your notes from here to kingdom come. Trying to reorganize them on the spot can, well, put you on the spot.

Just remember, whatever format you prefer, be sure to use it. Without the outline, your speech will take shape like concrete poured without forms. It will flow everywhere - which is to say it will go nowhere.

Periu's Point

A speech should be exactly as long as it needs to be and not a second longer, but a good rule of thumb is 20 minutes. That time fits most of the business club formats well. It's also a good timetable for most business or organizational presentations. Each situation has a different time frame. For example, keynote speeches run 45 minutes. Educational speeches are generally 1 ½ hours to four hours, and workshops can last an entire day, two days, three days or even more.

Points of Departure

How many points should a speech include? The answer is, of course, "that depends." How many points do you really need to make? Equally important, how many points can your audience absorb in a single presentation? Overloading your audience undermines your purpose. Focus on your intent - always.

You'll hear different opinions from various experts in the field. My recommendation is a range of three to five points per speech. That's not to say that you can't have six or seven or that you can't have just one. Three to five is a rule of thumb, but it's a good one and one that's been proven over time. Remember the KISS rule - Keep It Simple, Stupid. I'm making a slight modification to that statement. For the purposes of this book, any further references to the KISS rule are in reference to Keep It Simple, Speaker.

Begin At The End

You have to know where you're going before you can find the right road to get you there. Again, what is the 25-words or less intent of your presentation? Think about the end. Once you know your stopping point, you can select your best point of departure and the most logical points along the way to illustrate that goal. Never make a speech just to make a speech. Always have a good point. What is your purpose? One of your goals should always be to make sure your audi-

ence gets real value from your presentation. I've known managers
who never think about their weekly sales meeting until just before it
begins. That's unforgivable. A manager should invest a minimum of
15 minutes a day for that weekly meeting.

A meeting isn't a chore; it's an opportunity and too many managers
waste it. I've actually witnessed a sales manager fall asleep during his
own presentation. What kind of motivation does that sad behavior
encourage?

I also believe in the old military rule. "Tell 'em what you're going to
tell 'em. Tell 'em and then tell 'em what you just told 'em." Regardless
of how well-educated or experienced your audience might be, never
assume that they have or understand all the information you have.
Something that's downright obvious to you may have little or no
meaning to an audience without your experience or education.

> "Who thinks an inch, but talks a yard,
> needs a kick in the foot."
> Chinese Proverb

Speech Formats

A speech isn't limited to, "Hello. Here I am. This is why I'm speaking. Vote for me. Thanks. Goodbye." You can construct your outline
to fit a number of very effective formats. Which one you choose will
depend upon the needs dictated by the subject matter, the needs of
the audience, and your personal style. You can find a lot of material
on these formats at your library or neighborhood bookstore. Here's a
list of my favorites.

Chronological. Outline your presentation according to the timeline in which relevant events occurred or will occur. "We launch the
new product Thursday at 8 a.m. Eastern time. When the news
reports are published that evening, we will meet to begin an evaluation..."

Problem/Solution. State a problem and then provide your
answer. "Our costs of shipping our products from the East Coast
manufacturing plant to our distribution center in the Midwest is having a severe negative impact on our quarterly profits. By moving our

69

facility to the Chicago area we will reduce shipping costs, deliver product to customers faster, and improve our profit margins by five percent per quarter."

Cause/Effect. Here you state something that has happened and then what happened as a result of that action. "The Chicago move has already had a positive effect on our quarterly profit margins. Projections for the next year indicate..."

Theory/Practice. This reflects the frequently wide divergence between "book learning" and the real world. "While we can now move product faster from Chicago, the disruption in deliveries caused by our move has cost the company one of our biggest customers."

Expand on a Word. Find a commonly used word and adapt it to the keystone of your presentation. "I want you salespeople to get a piece of the pie. By that I mean P for plan, I for investigate, and E for execute."

Expand on a phrase. You can do the same thing with a phrase. When Shakespeare wrote, "Two stars keep not their motion in one sphere," he meant simply that two objects cannot occupy the same space. The same rule applies to management. Two bosses in one company is an unworkable management system in a competitive business environment.

Location Directed. Sometimes the physical location will dictate the format of your speech. For example, if you're giving a plant tour you might want to follow the process from unloading raw material through manufacturing, inspection, and shipment of the final product at the company railhead.

Examples. Take an example of one thing and use it to make your point about another. "Building a great company is like building a house. First you select your neighborhood, that's your product. Then draw up a blueprint, which is the manufacturing process. Next..."

Phrases. Select a phrase, current or even out of date, that makes your point. "The phrase 'Tell it like it is' was popular during the sixties, but it also applies to the inaccurate statements in our competitor's latest advertising campaign."

Winging it. As a rule, I don't recommend speaking without thorough preparation. Some very knowledgeable and confident speakers can pull it off and make their presentations soar, but for most of us it's a surefire way to crash and burn.

Q&A. I know a speaker who begins his presentation with, "Hello, I'm John Doe and that concludes my prepared remarks. We're now into the question and answer portion of our program." He then lets the audience questions direct the flow of his presentation.

Again, this format is not recommended for most of us. Winging it and the Q&A format leave open too many opportunities for disaster. These formats, to a limited extent, can be outlined. A good speaker will have some idea of where to start and where to proceed. Audience members may be shy about asking questions at first, and you'll need to start somewhere.

Each format is effective when used properly. I encourage you to experiment with as many as you are comfortable presenting. In fact, experiment with them all to determine your strengths and weaknesses and best presentation techniques. It's all part of knowing yourself so that you can know and relate better to your audience.

The outline is your self-drawn road map that gets you from beginning to end by the most practical, most convincing, and most powerful path. It is an essential initial step that can turn and average meeting into a great meeting as a direct result of a fearless speaker.

That's you.

THE ONE-MINUTE SUMMARY

- Outline every speech, even if you decide to use the winging it or the Q&A format. Lack of preparation is a sure way to fail in achieving your intent.
- An outline is your roadmap to a successful speech.
- Begin with the ending. Know where you are going when you start. That way the elements of your speech will naturally fall into place.
- State the purpose, the keystone, of your speech in 25 words or less.
- Use outline format that works best for you.
- Outline your speech so that it is precisely as long as it needs to be.
- Speech formats include: chronological, problem/solution, cause/effect, theory/practice, expand on a word, expand on a phrase, location directed, examples, phrases, winging it, and Q&A.

10

"When the ancients said a work well begun was half done, they meant to impress the importance of always endeavoring to make a good beginning."

Polybius

The Speech: The Beginning

The first three minutes of your speech are make-or-break moments. Many experts cut that figure in half and state that if you haven't hooked your audience in the first 90 seconds, you're already in troubled waters. Whichever time frame is accurate, and I lean toward the 90 second rule, the opening of your presentation is critical. It's like a headline in an ad. If you don't grab the audience's attention, they'll never bother to read the copy in the body of the ad. They won't be around to get your message.

This chapter is divided into two basic parts:
- The opening portion of your speech, and
- The opening portion of your presentation of that speech.

"Affairs are easier of entrance than exit; and it is but common prudence to see our way out before we venture in."

Aesop

> *"When giving a speech know where you're going before you even think about taking the first step. Like any sound military operation, you need an exit strategy."*
>
> Omar Periu

Part I. In The Beginning Was The Word

If you want to read a great speech, find a copy of *Julius Caesar* by William Shakespeare and examine Mark Antony's speech to the mob. Caesar has just been assassinated and the crowd is praising the assassins and cursing their former ruler. In one brilliant, well-constructed speech, Antony turns his audience's emotions 180 degrees. They mourn Caesar and begin lusting for the blood of his killers. It really is a beautiful example of fearless speaking.

"I come to bury Caesar, not to praise him," he says. This is called a hook. It's a device to grab your audience's attention immediately so that they'll stay with you and hear the rest of your words - the headline, so to speak. Antony was widely known as Caesar's favorite. The mob expected a long-winded speech about Caesar's greatness. Instead all they hear is "I just 'wanna bury the guy." You can almost hear a collective "Say what?" from the crowd. Of course, Antony has another intent in mind, but before he can get to it, he has to hook his audience. Intent is to begin with the end in mind. Know the results you want to achieve. Then go achieve them.

You have to do the same thing. Use your imagination. Think about what you want to say and then figure out a way to say it that will startle your audience into following you further. Make sure that whatever examples, stories or techniques you use can be directly applied to your subject. Here are a few idea starters.

Use current events. Instead of, "I want to talk about salesmanship," say, "The central message in the president's speech on military preparedness yesterday can be applied to our need to know not only our product, but the products of our competitors." Ask a question. Instead of, "Today we'll discuss retirement planning," say, "How many of you managers want to retire in comfort and style ten years ahead of schedule?"

Use statistics. Instead of, "It's time to reconsider our state's tax policies," say, "Fifty-five percent of the American people believe in UFOs. That's exactly double the number of people who believe in our recent proposals to place a tax on..."

Tell a personal story. Instead of, "We need increased safety in plant cleanup procedures," say "Last night my kid told me he was afraid of the boogieman in the dark. Folks, we have a boogieman in the dark right here. It's the undercapitalization of our expansion into the Southwestern markets."

I use a personal story often. I tell how my family and I arrived here from Cuba with nothing other than the shirts on our backs and now I'm living the American Dream. Each time I tell the story I tailor the presentation to the needs of my audience. For example, an inspirational speech might require a more emotional approach than a presentation for a leadership conference or a seminar on the challenges of being an entrepreneur.

Play a trick. I have an associate who teaches intuition to business audiences. He writes something on a piece of paper and asks, "What letter did I just write down?" After the individuals make their guesses, he holds up the paper, which has a number on it. His point is to teach them to avoid making assumptions. When playing tricks on your audience, make sure they are harmless and fun for all involved.

Involve the audience in your story. "You folks have all been uncomfortable on a crowded elevator, haven't you? That's because your personal space has been invaded, which brings me to the subject of controlling yourself with an unruly customer."

Use giveaways. People appreciate gifts, even if they're virtually worthless knickknacks purchased from an advertising specialty company. This grabs attention and creates a sense of obligation in the audience. Since you have given something, they have an obligation to give you their attention in return.

Quote a quote. Instead of, "We should expand our markets," say, "William Hazlitt said, 'Great thoughts reduced to practice become great acts.' Folks, we've been thinking of expanding into the Pacific Rim for some time. Now is the time to put our thoughts into practice and achieve a great act."

You get the point. Use your imagination. Think of clever, even brilliant ways to start your speech. Think about your audience and what might appeal to their sense of humor, sense of civic duty, self-interest, company pride, or whatever motivation is appropriate. Open your presentation with something that will open their eyes and keep them open. Once you've got your audience hooked, you can safely move on to the body of the speech, secure that your audience is making the journey with you.

Periu's Point

There are many ways to ruin your opening remarks. Among the most effective are beginning with an apology, telling a story or making an example that does not apply to your topic, dragging out your presentation, and failing to double check your audio/visual aids which inevitably blow up in your face. Ruining your opening remarks can leave your entire presentation in ruins.

Part II.
In The Beginning Was The Spoken Word

Now that you've outlined or written your opening remarks, it's time to speak them. You have a number of challenges to overcome in the first 90 seconds to three minutes of your presentation:

#1. Build rapport.
#2. Get the audience on your side.
#3. Show respect.
#4. Prove that you're worthy of their time.

Build Rapport

One of your first duties is to build rapport with your audience. Mark Antony did this wonderfully with his, "Friends, Romans, countrymen, lend me your ears." Notice the brilliance of that. We're all friends and fellow citizens of the great empire. We're in this together.

When he says "lend" he's asking permission and at the same time showing respect for those countrymen. Having built a rapport with his audience, he begins to ease, carefully, slowly and gently, into the body of his presentation.

Get The Audience On Your Side

Most audiences want to cheer for the speaker, so you actually begin about halfway to your goal. As they say in politics, the battle is yours to lose. One of the best techniques is to begin your speech on time. This shows that you are a man or woman of your word, that you are professional, and that you respect the time other people have granted you. One of the best ways to build rapport is to express how much of an honor it is to speak to the group and then tell them why it's such an honor.

I like to show up early and stay late if at all possible. Meeting people before the speech gives you the opportunity to build a number of relationships. By the time you make the presentation, many of the people think of you as "one of us." Staying around after the speech can have the same effect and, one-on-one, you might make a few more converts from among those who weren't convinced by your presentation.

Show Respect

A speaker can't just say "I respect you folks." He or she has to prove it. Show your respect for the audience by being prepared for the audience. Make sure the room is set up properly, that the air conditioning/heating will be at the correct temperature for a room full of people, that your appearance is appropriate, and that all your AV equipment is in working order. "Excuse me, folks, while I plug this in" shows a lack of respect and breaks up your presentation. You may never recover.

Prove You're Worthy Of Their Time

Only the completed speech (and the ensuing "hoorays") can totally prove that. But you can, and must, begin proving the point from the very beginning. Be prepared. Know your stuff. Express the correct demeanor for your presentation. In other words, don't be too cute or humorous for a serious speech. Don't be too serious about a subject that naturally lends itself to humor.

Periu's Point

Many speakers use or attempt to use humor to help build and maintain rapport with an audience. Humor is a great tool when properly used. Make sure that any joke, funny story or comment applies to the topic of your speech. Regardless of how funny it may be, if a joke doesn't fit the subject, it will throw off your audience. You'll not be able to make your initial points because they'll be trying to figure out the non-existent meaning of your joke.

A good technique is to note your credentials. Why are you the one making this speech? What makes you so special or so knowledgeable? The audience is probably wondering about this, so tell them. Don't brag, but it's perfectly okay to let them know why you have the right to make your presentation. Of course, you can also do the same thing by seeing that the person who introduces you explains your credentials. Your audience is in place to hear your pearls of wisdom. Do all that you can to make sure they shine. Your audience wants and deserves the genuine article.

Solid preparation of your opening followed by a sound delivery sets the stage for the next two stages: the body of your speech and the closing. All that follows depends upon the foundation you build. That's why the first 90 seconds to three minutes are so crucial. Plan it. Practice it. Deliver it with the force of your convictions as did Mark Antony. Then at the conclusion of your speech you can say, as did Antony, "Fortune is merry, and in this mood will give us anything."

"Words, like eyeglasses, blur everything that they do not make more clear."
Joseph Joubert

THE ONE- MINUTE SUMMARY

- Use the first 90 seconds to three minutes of your presentation effectively and with care. They are make-or-break moments.
- Hook your audience with an attention-grabbing opening remark. Grab their attention immediately so they'll hold onto your every word.
- Good opening techniques include: using current events, asking a question, using statistics, telling a personal story, playing a trick, involving the audience in a story, using giveaways, and quoting a quote.
- Plan your opening remarks with extreme care. You can ruin a speech by beginning with an apology, telling a story or making an example that does not apply to your topic, dragging out your presentation, and failing to double check your audio/visual aids.
- It is essential that you use your opening moments to build rapport, get the audience on your side, show respect, and prove that you're worthy of your audience's time.
- Begin your speech with the end in mind.

The One Minute Meeting

11

> *"On speaking, first have something to say, second say it, third stop when you have said it, and finally, give it an accurate title."*

John Shaw Billings

The Speech: The Middle

The three main parts of your speech, beginning, middle and end, are equally important. Blow one and you've probably blown your entire speech or at least done it considerable harm toward achieving your intent. The middle section, however, has to carry most of the burden because that is where you'll place most of the information. The middle, sometimes called the body, should flow naturally from the beginning and should just as naturally flow into the ending. This is where you deliver those three to seven key points mentioned earlier. Don't be intimidated. Chances are that huge gulf of time you think you have to fill isn't nearly as wide as you believe. Just break down the process into manageable bits and pieces. For example, let's say you have a 20 minute presentation to the management team. Allow a minute or so for introductions and greetings, then three minutes for introduction to your speech, a minute or so for the ending, and then say five minutes to answer questions. The time allotted for the main body of your presentation is now about 10 minutes. If you have five key points to make, that's only two minutes per point. Two minutes is about the length of the average commercial break on network television - about the time it takes you to grab a glass of water, a couple of cookies, sit back down in your evening chair, and flick through the channels once before your favorite show comes back on. In other words, not much time at all.

Hadn't you better use that limited time to your best advantage?

Periu's Point

If you're going to write a speech, write it. I once met a fellow working on a motion picture screenplay. He was "committed" to seeing it completed as soon as he finished his outline and research. A year later he was still researching and outlining and had yet to write word number one on the actual script. That was years ago and I bet he's still committed...and still researching and outlining. And still without a finished product. Don't procrastinate. Do your research and your outlining, but then be sure to start writing.

Tell 'Em

You've told 'em what you were going to tell 'em during your opening. Now it's time to actually say what you've come to say. You have already chosen a format: chronological, problem/solution, cause/effect, theory/practice, expanding on a word, expanding on a phrase, location directed, examples, phrases, winging it, or Q&A. Ideally, you have avoided the last two until your are experienced enough to handle those tricky formats.

You also know your key points. Your responsibility is to make those points clearly, with conviction, and with appropriate explanation and support. You will engage all the tools in your toolbox as appropriate to the situation. You'll conquer your fear of speaking. You'll be logical, emotional, aloof, involved, humorous and heartbreaking. You'll use eye contact and body language. You'll tell stories, bring up examples, insert quotations, statistics and back-up materials to support your case. You'll involve the audience, taking their questions and perhaps even asking a few of your own. Throughout your speech you'll be focused on the intent of your presentation. All of this, of course, will be planned and rehearsed in advance.

The middle of your presentation is where you shine as a fearless speaker. This is where you convince your audience or fall flat on your face. The result is a matter of your own choosing. Prepare well, rehearse diligently, and deliver with conviction. Stay focused and you will prevail.

> *"Point of view must mean more than mere prejudice; it should express conclusions reached by that painful process known as thinking. And when new facts or factors are presented, free men should be as vigilant to change their viewpoints as to confirm them."*
>
> A. Mortimer Astbury

Too Much Of The Good Stuff

Down South folks have an expression, "too much of the good stuff," which is generally a reference to eating too much. Over time the meaning has been expanded. For example, a hangover from good Tennessee 'sipin whiskey is too much of the good stuff. You can give your audience a hangover if your speech provides too much of the good stuff. Have you ever attended a speech, a management orientation, or a sales presentation during which the speaker has made his or her point and convinced, converted or sold the audience only to keep on speaking until that audience is lost? That's too much of the good stuff. It's a sin. It shows a lack of respect for your audience, and, worst of all, it's a sure way to fail to achieve the intent of your speech.

The ancient Greek playwright Euripides wrote that moderation is "the noblest gift of heaven." A good speech is focused. Like a well-edited book or motion picture, all the "fat" has been cut away, leaving only the best material. Only inexperienced speakers try to fit everything into a single presentation. That's a sure way to lose everything you want to achieve. Whenever you make a speech, always consider your audience and give them the "noblest gift." Give them everything you've got - in moderation.

> *"Speeches that are measured by the hour will die with the hour."*
> Thomas Jefferson

Make The Transition

A speech should have a natural flow to it. One topic or one area of a topic should flow easily and logically into the next. An audience shouldn't have to pause and shift gears only to get lost trying to figure out where the speaker has just jumped. Transitions help keep your audience riding in the vehicle of your speech. A good transition eases your audience from point number one to point number two and beyond without confusion.

Remember, your audience may not have your level of knowledge or experience on the subject at hand. They certainly don't have your unique position or viewpoint. The move from point A to point B may be logical to you, but that jump may seem totally illogical to someone else. Smooth transitions help assure that everyone sees the logic of your argument. They keep everyone on board and up to speed.

A Few Words In The Right Place

I recommend, highly, that you use the active instead of the passive voice. For example, which sentence has more power:

Passive: The board of directors was addressed by your author.

Active: I addressed the board of directors.

In the active voice, the subject of the sentence provides the action, as in the title of a successful motion picture comedy from some years back, "I'm 'Gonna Get You, Sucker!'" Imagine the drawing power of that same movie had its title used the passive voice. "You, Sucker, Will Be Gotten By Me!" The active voice is more active, aggressive and to the point.

Get the point?

Keeping It Simple, Speaker

Jargon and the use of over-inflated, overly sophisticated, and overly important sounding words seem to have a stranglehold on American speech. "We strive to utilize a variety of techniques to accomplish a broad spectrum of results toward the bottom line in order to enhance stockholder value through strategic business initiatives by empowered employees working in new team paradigms." That type of gibberish is attractive to some speakers, but its effect upon an audience is to cause a collective "Say what?"

Show respect for your audience. If you're addressing an audience of technicians and if your subject is technical, then it's okay to use commonly understood jargon, acronyms, and insider language. Generally, your audiences will understand and respond best to plain, old English. You're not making a speech to impress people. You're making a speech to be understood, to convince an audience, and achieve a specific intent. Speak clearly and don't trip over the paradigms.

> *"Spartans, stoics, heroes, saints and gods use a short and positive speech."*
> Ralph Waldo Emerson
>
> *"'Short, sweet 'n hard to beat' is a formula that has worked for poets, playwrights, authors and speakers for thousands of years. Take heed."*
> Omar Periu

Prove Your Point

Supporting documentation is important and in some speeches essential. There's a fundamental rule of advertising and marketing: a statement without accompanying proof is perceived by the audience as a mere claim and nothing more. Proof makes it real.

Proof of your arguments can come in many forms: statistics, historical events, true life stories, your own life experiences, quotes from knowledgeable sources, and in your audio/visual aids. There are two guidelines that have served me well in preparing documentation for my speeches. These are:

#1. Be specific. Make sure your supporting material really does support your claim(s). Piling up statistics, statements or stories just for the sake of volume is an example of "too much of the good stuff."

#2. Share the wealth. You have a wealth of support materials, so why not use several different types. Some people will respond logically to dry statistics. Others will react more favorably to an emotional approach, such as a personal story.

Speaking of emotions...

Choosing Logic Vs. Emotion

Which approach is best, a logical or an emotional one? As you might expect, the answer is "that depends." The question can best be answered with another question. Which approach will best meet the needs of your next audience and take you closer to achieving your intent?

Some attendees will respond best to an A+B=C approach. Like Detective Joe Friday, they want "just the facts, ma'am" and nothing more. For example, if you're pushing the proposition to fix a mass of potholes downtown, your logical approach might address the increased cost of repairs and new tires for the consumers in that neighborhood, the city's continuing expense of temporary repairs, and the negative effects of bad streets on tourism.

Other folks respond best to the emotional appeal. In the case of the downtown potholes you might then speak about the unfair burden of those expenses on the poor working people who have to drive those streets. These are families sacrificing food, clothing and school supplies to get the front ends of their cars realigned and to buy new tires. It's just not fair.

Most likely, your audience will be made up of a mix of types. Why not mix it up yourself? You can combine both approaches. Lead off with the facts and figures to reach the logical thinkers. Then wrap things up with an emotional approach to grab the other half of the audience. That way you get the best of both worlds. So does your audience.

THE ONE-MINUTE SUMMARY

- Treat the beginning, middle and end of your speech with equal care. Each must lead to the achievement of your intent.
- The middle carries the burden of information.
- Write out every speech. Don't get so bogged down in research and outlining that you never put words to paper.
- Use all the appropriate speaking tools to make your points.
- Use only relevant information. Don't provide so much data that your audience loses your key points.
- Use transitions to make sure your audience stays with you from beginning to end.
- Provide support for your claims to make them logical statements.
- Use logic, emotion or combine them to reach different personalities.

12

"I am not afraid of tomorrow, for I have seen yesterday and I love today."

William Allen White

The Speech: End

Making a great speech is like living a great life. There's a solid past (opening), a productive midlife (middle) leading to a successful future (ending). Yesterday, today and tomorrow lead naturally from one point to the next. A fearless speaker always ends his or her presentation with a well-prepared and rehearsed closing. To do otherwise severely diminishes the intended results of your speech. Ending without a closing is also an insult to your audience. It's like telling a joke without including the punch line.

Regardless of its length, the ending has equal weight of importance with the beginning and middle of your presentation. Neglect it at your peril. Sarah J. Duncan wrote, "If you have anything of importance to tell me, for God's sake begin at the end." The ending is the intent you aim for throughout your entire speech. Make sure your audience knows where you're going in the beginning, that they stay with you through the middle, and that they're with you at the end (screaming, shouting, applauding, and praising).

Sometimes however, events are out of our hands. I was hired to address a company once. The owner, the old man, didn't know me, but his son had heard me and thought I could contribute to his organization. Unfortunately, the dad didn't really believe in training. Through no fault of my own we got off to a late start. I was in the middle of my presentation when good 'ol dad stands up and announces that it's "happy hour." Seeing the handwriting on the wall, I tried to wrap up quickly, but I wasn't even allowed that courtesy. "Son, we're through. It's happy hour," he said.

Well, dad got his happy hour. I got a very sincere apology from the son, but the employees never got to hear my full presentation.

Wrap It Up

The ending should briefly and succinctly summarize your three, five or seven key points. For example, "In closing I'd like you to remember four key points about my proposed plant safety rule: one, entry into confined spaces should always be considered a potentially life-threatening task; two, we have had more than eight medical situations in this area within the past year; three, we should establish a mandatory policy of atmospheric testing prior to entering any confined space on our facility; and four, as managers it is our fiscal and moral duty to our employees and our shareholders to adopt this policy. Any questions?"

Notice how the speaker not only wrapped up the key points, but also reminded the audience of his or her opinion of the matter ("...potentially life-threatening..."). The relationships between each point were clearly expressed. And there was a call to action. That's just a brief example. In the real world, the speaker would have had a moment or two more to toss in some support data or a good quote.

Periu's Point
A typical ending should be about ten to fifteen percent of your entire speech. That's just enough time to cover the essential points and to leave them feeling a sense of satisfactory completion.

Step Up To A Great Ending

Here are six steps I've used over the years to help build great endings to my presentations. Follow this plan. Adapt it to the needs of your presentation and to the needs of your audience. The ending isn't just a stopping point. It's where you "close the sale" with your audience and they accept the intent of your speech as their own.

Step #1. Think about it. Before you write the first word, visualize the ending of your presentation. Think about the desired reaction. Do you want laughter? Tears? Cheers? Serious thought? Signing a petition? See that conclusion clearly and only then start creating it.

Step #2. Write it down. Some folks write their speeches word for word. Others use notes or speak extemporaneously. Whichever format you prefer, choose it and then use it. Put your words on paper, computer disc, or notepad.

Step #3. Practice. Practice may not always make perfect, but it does make for a better delivery. Pay special attention to timing. You don't want to cut it so short that the audience doesn't realize your presentation is over. You don't want to ramble on so long that the audience is praying for an ending, either.

Step #4. Build the ending into the middle. Prepare your audience for the close. "I want to make this point before wrapping up." "My last, but not least concern is..." "In conclusion..." This is a bit of tell 'em what you're 'gonna tell 'em" right before you tell 'em what you just told 'em.

Step #5. Close with a "zinger." A zinger is a snappy one-line, final sentence or phrase. It can be humorous or heartbreaking, depending upon the needs of the situation. Think long and hard about your last words. "If you leave here with only one thought, I want that thought to be..." Think of the closing zinger as an ignition switch to turn on the applause from your audience.

Always give your audience more, especially when they're not expecting more. Close your presentation, accept the applause, and then give them a little something else. Such as...

Step #6. Always hold a question and answer session. If there's no time built into the program, offer to stick around for an informal session. There's a great strategy night club singers use rather effectively. It's been honed to a fine art in Las Vegas. At the conclusion of a performance, the entertainer pauses and tells the crowd that they are something special and that there's something magic in the air. The singer then says he or she's going to keep on performing. Only repeat customers and music critics note that this "something special" happens every performance. It's not a crass technique. The singer really does make the night special by providing something extra, even if that extra has been planned into the performance. You can do the same thing with a Q&A session.

> *"All's well that ends well."*
> William Shakespeare

End With A Bang

T.S. Elliot wrote, "This is the way the world ends, not with a bang but a whimper." Well, the world can end whichever way it chooses, but you had better choose bang over whimper to end your speech. There are a number of proven techniques. Here are some of my favorites.

Bookend Your Presentation. By that I mean close with a reference to your beginning. If you asked, "What shall we do about the proposed move to the Pacific Rim markets" in your opening, close with the answer to that question. If you started with a quote, a story, a statistic or whatever, then wrap up your presentation with a reference, a bold one, to that opening.

Question Your Audience. After making your presentation, let your audience supply the answer you want them to adopt. "Are we going to continue allowing our chief competitor unchallenged access to Pacific Rim markets, or are we ready, willing and able to make the acquisition in Indonesia this year? Are we up to the challenge?"

Quote A Poem. The world has produced poetic geniuses since before the era of recorded language. Those poets wouldn't mind a bit of extra publicity now and then. Just make sure your poem is more than eloquent. It must be appropriate to the occasion.

"I favor legal freedoms,
such as that of speech,
But there's a need of substance
Something more than screech."

Art Buck

Close With A Story. Again the story should be appropriate to the subject of your speech and to your audience. A story can be funny, bring tears to the eye, or merely illustrative. Stories are everywhere. Keep an eye out when watching the television news, reading your favorite newspaper or magazine, or just in everyday conversation. The libraries are full of books filled with useful stories. You don't have to pore over hundreds of pages of biographies either. The "Chicken Soup" book series, for example, is a wonderful source of good stories.

Make A Call To Action. Ask your audience to take some kind of action: buy that plant in Indonesia, increase the sales commission, move to a new facility, create a new product or service, launch a new public relations campaign, or whatever course of action is needed to further the cause of your speech. A call to action can be in the form of a request. "I'm asking you to vote 'yes' on the plant expansion budget." It can be in the form of a command, too. "Don't waste another moment. Vote yes today. Act now!"

Gaze Into A Crystal Ball. Predict the outcome of your speech or of some action or inaction. "If we do not acquire this new property, our chief competitor will achieve market dominance within three years." In Conclusion...

Generally, the audience remembers the ending more than any other part of the speech. Of course, the effectiveness of that ending depends upon the effectiveness of the opening and the middle, but more than anything else, the audience will walk away carrying your final words. Make them good ones. No, be fearless and make them great!

THE ONE-MINUTE SUMMARY

- Start out by knowing precisely where you are going. The ending is of equal importance as the beginning and middle of your speech.
- Summarize your key points briefly in your wrap up. Tell 'em what you just told 'em.
- An ending should be approximately ten to fifteen percent of the speech.
- Use the six steps toward building a great ending: think, write, practice, tell the audience that the ending is approaching, close with a "zinger," and hold a Q&A session.
- Create an ending with real impact. Good ending techniques include: "bookending," posing a question, quoting a poem, telling a story, making a call to action, and making a prediction.

13

> "It is an excellent rule
> to be observed in all
> discussions, that men
> should give soft words
> and hard arguments;
> that they should not so
> much strive to silence
> or vex, as to convince
> their opponents."
>
> J. Harold Wilkins

Development And Rehearsing

Now that you've written the beginning, middle and ending, you still have a few chores before you. A writer friend of mine says that the art of writing is in the first draft, but the crafting of the work is in the re-write. The first draft of your speech is only that, a first step. To finish the journey successfully, you have to take many more.

A diamond roughed into shape, still requires polishing. Before stepping in front of your audience, be sure to add some polish to your presentation. Here are a few tips on how to make that speech really shine.

Read It Out Loud

Before you begin revising, take an honest look at what you've done in the first draft. First, read it straight through without stopping to take notes. Time it just to see how close you've come to reaching your time limit. At this point, you're not rewriting, you're just getting a feel for what you can keep, what you should revise, and what you should toss out the nearest window.

Go through the speech again. This time note any weaknesses:
- Lack of focus on intent.
- Precise words and phrases that can be made stronger.
- Use of the passive voice that should be changed to active voice.
- Jargon, terms or acronyms that need immediate explanation.
- Clichés, shopworn terms, or out of date expressions.
- Unnecessary repetition.
- Obscure references or stories.

Periu's Point

Don't let the length of your speech keep you from revising it. Break the development of your presentation into three stages: (1) planning the speech, (2) writing the speech, (3) re-writing and polishing the speech.

Q&A Yourself

A good way to review your presentation is to put yourself in the place of an audience member. How does your speech stack up from that point of view?

Is my language clear and concise? Mark Twain said, "I never write 'metropolis' for seven cents, because I can get the same money for 'city.'" Are you using big words when little ones will do a better job? Keep your words and phrases short, sweet and hard to beat. With very rare exceptions, you'll do a better job speaking just the way people speak every day.

Do my sentences run on and on? The printed message allows for numerous breaks and asides within a single sentence. Try that in a speech and you'll lose half your audience. Break long sentences into shorter, easier to understand sentences. A good rule of thumb is to keep your sentences at 20 words or less. The longer your sentences, the shorter the attention span of your audience.

Is my wording precise? For example, you could say "We need to make some more sales around here, don't 'ya think?" Or you could say, "A new bonus plan will revitalize our sales force while increasing morale and year-to-date sales." What do you really want to say? Don't beat around the bush or be vague. Say it!

Am I being pompous? Trying to show off generally comes off as arrogance. Pomposity can sneak into your presentation in a number of forms. Referring to yourself as "we" is a perfect example. The unnecessary use of foreign phrases is another one. Why use a false French accent to say "faiare etalage" when the American phrase "show off" will do? Don't let obscure abbreviations or jargon slip into your presentation. As a real estate professional addressing a group of prospects, you may understand that FHLMC means Federal Home Loan Mortgage Corporation or that the CAI is the Community Associations Institute, but if you use those acronyms without expla-nation on an audience unfamiliar with industry terms, you'll proba-bly drown your audience in the alphabet soup. "Showboating" for an audience doesn't elevate your position. It just builds barriers between you and the people you want to motivate.

> *"It is but a poor eloquence which only shows that the orator can talk."*
> Sir Joshua Reynolds

Avoid A Speech That Sounds Memorized

I'm not saying don't memorize your speech. You should always memorize your speech, but it should sound spontaneous. The key is to know your subject matter so well that you can go from the heart to a basic structure. The thought of speaking without reading your speech as you go may frighten some of you, but believe me that's a sure fire road to disaster. Know it in your heart. Speak from your heart and earn the desired heartfelt response.

I attended a marketing presentation during which one of the par-ticipants made his presentation word-for-word from his hand written notes. Unfortunately, at one point he had reached the bottom of a page in mid sentence and had to continue on the next page. You guessed it. When he came to the break, he broke his speech until he turned the page. The moment was awkward not only for the speaker, but for the audience. He never recovered his momentum after that.

A recited speech sounds robotic. There's just no way you can make a point or move an audience that way. You must sound natural, excited and committed. How you say what you say communicates a specific message to your audience. They'll never get excited if you sound like you're reciting a list of presidents for your fourth grade teacher.

Know your subject inside and out, backwards and forwards. Write a good outline or series of brief notes for reference. Write your speech. Memorize it and practice often, so that it sounds unrehearsed. A successful speech is made from heart to heart and from soul to soul.

> *"Order means light and peace, inward liberty and free command over one's self; order is power."*
> Henri Frederic Amiel

Practice Mentally Ten Times

You'll find a common mental thread among the top performers in all professional sports. The best of them "play" the game before they step out on the court, diamond, field or course. Golf great Jack Nicklaus is famous for this practice. He not only "plays" the entire course before a game, he mentally practices each stroke along the way. He visualizes the ball, his swing, and where the ball will land.

I do exactly the same thing before my presentations. I "make" my speech at least ten times in my mind before I ever step up to the lectern. I highly recommend this practice. You'll be amazed at how much improvement you can make, not only in the speech itself, but also in your presentation.

The bottom line in the development and rehearsal phase of preparing your speech is simple. Your prime directive is to make sure that the speech is your speech. Make sure that it says what you want it to say in the way you want it said. Now, let's move on to the next two chapters and see how we put all your hard work into action.

THE ONE-MINUTE SUMMARY

- Always invest the time to polish your completed speech.
- Read your speech out loud to discover: weak words and phrases; use of the passive voice; unexplained jargon, terms or acronyms; clichés, shopworn terms, and out of date expressions; unnecessary repetition; obscure references, stories, etc.
- Constantly ask yourself if you're really achieving your intent.
- Divide your speech-making into three areas: planning, re-writing and polishing.
- Make your language clear and concise.
- Avoid run on sentences.
- Be precise.
- Avoid pomposity.
- Know your material so well that your memorized presentation sounds spontaneous.
- Practice your speech mentally ten times.

14

"Good management consists in showing average people how to do the work of superior people."

John D. Rockefeller

Meeting Mechanics

This chapter isn't about getting to know the guys down at the neighborhood garage. It's about the mechanics of conducting a great meeting. You can't play unless you know the rules of the game and you certainly can't lead without mastering them. Here are some of the challenges and opportunities you'll face (and master) as a meeting leader and fearless speaker.

"Mr. Chairman?"

Or Ms. or Mrs. Chairman, as the case may be, has a number of responsibilities in seeing that the meeting is run efficiently. As a chairperson, you will be managing one of two basic types of meetings. As the leader of an informal meeting your job is to make sure that the meeting is run in an orderly manner and that all attendees have the opportunity to speak. The chairperson of an informal meeting doesn't usually take sides on the issues at hand. He or she often refrains from participating in the debate.

The leader of a formal meeting, such as a board of directors meeting, is often governed by a number of specific rules. Publicly held companies, government bodies, and other organizations will have a set of guidelines that must be followed if the meeting is to be considered legitimate. In addition to keeping the meeting on track, the leader's responsibilities will be to make certain that all the rules and regulations are followed to the letter.

Regardless of whether the meeting is formal or informal, you have a number of responsibilities:

- Officially open the meeting.
- State the agenda.
- Keep the discussion focused on the topic at hand.
- Restate any motions.
- Follow rules and regulations.
- Control or dismiss any unruly attendants.
- Summarize the meeting at its conclusion.
- Close the meeting according to proper procedure.

> *"Leadership is the initiation and direction of endeavor in the pursuit of consequence. Anything else is criticism from janitors."*
> Royal Alcott

Organize Your Meeting

Every meeting will of course be different from every other meeting, yet there are some clear and proven guidelines you can follow for conducting just about any meeting. Here are six basic steps.

Step #1. Formally open the meeting. Sounds unnecessary, doesn't it, but a formal opening is essential. If you don't let everyone know that the meeting has begun, inevitably someone(s) won't hear or understand you and you'll have to backtrack later on so he or she can catch up. Be sure to follow all appropriate rules, regulations or bylaws to make sure your meeting is legitimate.

Step #2. Read and approve the minutes. Memories are fallible. It's important to read the minutes from the previous meeting to make sure everyone is on track and stays on track. Ask for a show of hands to approve the minutes so that later on no one can claim that he or she disagreed with the decisions. In many cases reading of the minutes is a mere formality, but it is an important formality nonetheless.

Step #3. Conduct the business of the meeting. You have an agenda for your meeting. Follow it step by step and deviate only if there is an overriding reason. Achieving your intent should rule all decisions.

Allow time for discussion and then take a vote on the matter at hand. Record the decision in your meeting minutes.

Step #4. Accept motions. Allow time for participants to make any motions (a statement of a proposed action). In more formal meetings these may have to be in writing and presented before the meeting. If such motions are on the agenda, you should follow the order as they appear. A chairman cannot withdraw a motion unless first obtaining permission from the individual making it.

Motions may be amended. If someone proposes an amendment, treat it as if it were a motion. Discuss the matter. Vote on the amendment. Then move back to the original motion.

When considering a motion, allow time to conduct enough discussion of the matter. Then call for a vote. Motions need to be seconded by someone other than the person making the motion. If there is no second then presumably there is no interest in the matter and you can move on to the next item on the agenda. Record the vote on each motion in your minutes.

If the motion is passed, it becomes a resolution - a written statement of the action to be taken.

Step #5. Ask for any further business. Some item of importance may have come up between the time the agenda was distributed and the meeting. Ask if there is any further business that the group needs to discuss. If so, continue the meeting.

Step #6. Close the meeting. Again, this is a formality, but a necessary one. Once you're sure that all business has been conducted, ask for a motion to close the meeting. Generally, you won't have any problems getting one. Ask and obtain a second to the motion. When a majority votes in favor of the motion, close the meeting.

> *"Conductors of great symphony orchestras do not play every musical instrument, yet through leadership the ultimate production is an expressive and unified combination of tones."*
> Thomas D. Bailey

> *"You wouldn't want to use a screwdriver to change a light bulb. Always have the right tools for the job in your speaker's 'toolbox.'"*
>
> Omar Periu

Great Expectations

A great leader is expected to act according to certain guidelines. For example, he or she is expected to manage the meeting in an efficient and fair manner. A great leader should also have great expectations for the group. Often the leader will have to "grow" the group into an effective unit. I recommend you set those expectations by using two key practices.

First, lead by example. Leaders who do not "practice what they preach" do not remain leaders for very long. Sure, they may retain the title, but their effectiveness in getting things accomplished becomes virtually nil.

Second, let your group know your intent and expectations. I think you would be surprised, if not amazed, at how many leaders do not let their followers know what is expected of them. Let your people know that they are expected to be fully prepared for every meeting. You go to the trouble of preparing an agenda, so each attendee should make the basic effort of becoming familiar with it. Any tasks assigned to be completed prior to the meeting should be wrapped on time. Any responsibilities for the meeting, such as delivering a report or bringing some materials, should be met. "Oh, shoot. I forgot" is not an acceptable reason for failure. If participants cannot make the meeting, you should be notified and be given a reason in advance.

Let your team know that you encourage questions, especially when someone doesn't understand a key point. Everyone is expected to contribute, but you frown on speaking just for the sake of hearing one's voice. Each member has a responsibility to leave the meeting fully informed. Also, let them know that aggressive debate, open and above board, is welcomed, but you will not tolerate discourtesy or a lack of respect for any member of the group. No one will be allowed to dominate the discussions, including the group leader.

Periu's Point

Here's a simple yet effective technique for when things appear to be getting out of hand. Stand up or move two steps toward the person or persons conversing before you address the situation. The action will provide a temporary distraction from the heated conversation and the added height gives you a psychological advantage. Remain calm, cool and collected, "let's discuss this at the Q&A session or break, thank you..." and continue, but be firm about getting back to the business at hand.

Disruptive behavior cannot be tolerated. Outbreaks of temper, lack of courtesy, talking out of turn and other such behaviors can ruin the effectiveness of any meeting. As a leader maintain control throughout the meeting, because if you don't it will be far more difficult to regain control and authority after you've lost it than it is to stay in charge in the first place.

The mechanics of successful meetings are basic, easy to understand, and generally easy to implement. A leader knows the rules and regulations and he or she follows them, setting a good example for the other members. The leader is firm (not dictatorial), fair, open, honest and willing to listen. A great leader also realizes that "a chain is only as strong as its weakest link" and that as a leader he or she must be the strongest link of all.

"You do not lead by hitting people over the head - that's assault, not leadership."
Dwight D. Eisenhower

105

THE ONE-MINUTE SUMMARY

- Know your organization's rules, regulations or bylaws of conducting meetings. Obey them so that your meeting is legitimate.
- A leader will conduct informal and/or formal meetings.
- A leader's responsibilities include opening the meeting, stating the agenda, keeping the discussion focused, restating motions, following rules and regulations, controlling or dismissing unruly attendants, summarizing the meeting at its conclusion, closing the meeting, and most importantly, making sure the meeting achieves its intent.
- Six basic steps for organizing a meeting are: formal opening, read and approve the minutes, conduct the business of the meeting, accept motions, ask for any further business, and close the meeting.
- A leader of time-effective meetings leads by example and sets a clear intent and a set of expectations for the group.
- Do not tolerate disruptive behavior. Be firm and fair, but always be in control.

15

> *"Enthusiasm is the greatest asset in the world. It beats money and power and influence. It is not more or less than faith in action."*
>
> Henry Chester

Inspiring Your Audience

Having an audience, and keeping an audience and motivating an audience are entirely different challenges. Most audiences will allow a speaker a grace period. They'll suspend their opinions to give the speaker a fair chance. This grace period is remarkably brief. That's why the first 90 seconds or so of your speech is so important. Your audience should be spellbound by your presentation. Think of Dr. Martin Luther King's incredible "I Have A Dream" speech, President John Kennedy's "Ask not what your country can do for you. Ask what you can do for your country," or even Patrick Henry's "Give me liberty or give me death." Those speakers knew how to grab an audience and motivate people.

It's A Matter Of Style

Every speaker, even a novice, has a personal style. You have a certain style. Of course, stumbling over phrases, mispronouncing words, losing your place and speaking timidly is a style of sorts. Your goal is to develop a style that is effective, fearless and focused. It may be dynamic, like a motivational guru, or be low key like a Gandi. The important matter is to develop and use your own style to the best of your abilities to inspire audiences.

Style is more important than many people realize. That's what puts the sizzle on the steak. I've read reports showing that the content of a

107

presentation accounts for just ten percent of the presentation's effect on an audience. Ninety percent of the effect results from the speaker's delivery. That's a frightening statistic in many ways, but it's one we as speakers have to take into consideration.

Possibly you could motivate an audience with a dull presentation, but that is very unlikely. Motivation requires inspiration. If you want to be an effective speaker, you have to have style. Let's look at some ways you can do that.

> *"A good style should show no signs of effort. What is written should seem a happy accident."*
> W. Somerset Maugham

> *"Of course, making something look effortless requires a considerable amount of effort."*
> Omar Periu

Dress For An Excess Of Success

The rule of thumb is to fit in with your audience as much as possible, to show them that you're one of the team or a member of the "family." Dress as your audience dresses. Give this some thought because different environments may radically alter the dress code. For example, if you're making an address to the nation's top CEOs in a plush corporate boardroom, a three-piece traditional business suit will probably be in order. If you're meeting that same group in a Phoenix luxury resort's clubhouse just before they tee off, shorts and a polo shirt may be entirely appropriate. If your presentation will be down on the manufacturing floor, coveralls and hard hats may be the dress of the day.

If you don't know your audience's likely attire, dress up. You can always dress down during your presentation. For example, suppose a speaker arrives in a dress suit for a presentation only to discover an entire audience in shirt sleeves. "You folks don't mind if I get a bit comfortable," he (or she) asks while removing the jacket. Within a few moments the tie can be removed, the collar opened and the long sleeves rolled up. Suddenly the over-dressed speaker has become one of the group.

Periu's Point

It's better to overdress than to under-dress. You must wear your "coat of authority" when making a presentation. After all, you are an authority. You should look the part.

Bodily Functions

Your body does more than cry, sneeze, belch and cough. Your body speaks, often more honestly and more expressively than the well-rehearsed words flowing from your mouth. There are many books available that cover the subject in-depth. I suggest that you acquire one, study it and incorporate the principles into your presentations.

How does body language "speak?" It's important to use your entire body. Speak with your words, but also with your hands, head and heart. Well, here are a few examples. If your arms are placed across your chest or on your hips and your feet are spread apart for balance, you are assuming a classical defensive posture. Your audience can perceive you as being defiant, uncommunicative or arrogant. Is that the impression you really want to make? On the other hand, if your arms are behind your back or if they're in front with your palms open, the audience will sense that you are confident, open and truthful.

Some of this is basic, such as nodding your head up and down to show approval or turning your head back and forth to show disbelief. You express yourself through body language all the time. From here on, however, I want you to think before you "speak" to make sure you're sending the appropriate messages. Here are a few suggestions.

Avoid:
- Unnatural, forced smiles. You fool no one.
- "Rocking the boat." Don't sway back and forth or side to side. It looks like you're dodging something.
- Sending negative messages, such as crossing your arms or rolling your eyes.
- Distractions, such as playing with a pencil on the lectern, glancing at your watch, etc.
- Recognizing someone by pointing with your finger. This is a classic no-no.

109

- Frozen posture. Lack of appropriate movement indicates a lack of conviction.

Adopt:

- A straight, confident stance.
- Natural body movements that communicate your true feelings. Think about how you act in normal conversation with a friend or associate and adapt those moves to an audience.
- Learn to smile naturally. (You can do this.)
- Move around, but with a purpose. A few years ago I observed a speaker on a stage before a large crowd. Wanting to address everyone equally, he moved back and forth between the far edges of the stage. He looked like a target in a video game. He should have addressed one side, made his point, moved to the other side for another point and then returned to the original side for his third point, etc.
- Use hand gestures, but don't be so repetitive that you look like a robot.
- Vary your speaking level according to the needs of your audience and the emotional content of your presentation. Raise and lower, speed up and slow down, and build in effective pauses.

All of these techniques will come to you in time. For now, I just want you to be aware of them. As a fearless speaker you have numerous audio/visual aids to help make your points. One of the most effective is your own beautifully expressive body.

Periu's Point

An English proverb states, "A smooth sea never made a skilled mariner." Realize now that you will inevitably stumble, flub your words, lose your place, provide a poor answer, forget some of the basics, and eventually break most or all the rules in the book. So what? As long as you have tried your best and learned something from the experience, you will continue to grow and improve. Great meeting-speakers aren't born. They are self-made.

Give 'Em An Earful With An Eyeful Of Contact

Eye contact is another highly effective form of body language. In one-on-one conversation, we maintain fairly steady eye contact with the other individual. That's not possible with a group of individuals, yet the speaker must make eye contact. It's a poor idea to sweep your eyes across the audience like searchlights over the ocean. That's not real eye contact even if you scan the audience row by row.

The best policy is to pick out one individual and focus on that person. Don't dwell on that individual throughout your entire speech because you'll be ignoring, rather obviously, the rest of your audience. Pick out one person, speak to him or her while you make a Point, and then move on to another and another and then another. About ten to twenty seconds per person is enough time. Of course, if you're taking questions, your problem is solved because you'll be looking at the person doing the asking.

Pardon the pun, but if you want to make a successful presentation, remember, "The eyes have it."

Periu's Point

You can't please everyone in an audience. Focus your attention and your energy on the attendees giving you positive feedback, such as nodding their heads in agreement, smiling, paying close attention, etc. Avoid negative people in the audience. In fact, that's a pretty good rule for life in general. Avoid the negatives.

Enthusiasm, Your Greatest Asset

I experienced an eye-opening event when preparing to go on stage for a presentation. I was in the corridors or backstage waiting to be called to the stage when a group of people came over and introduced themselves. We spoke briefly. As they were walking away I heard one woman say, "Well! He's doesn't seem very motivating." She didn't realize that my mental warm up for the presentation is to create focus on the task ahead. I also say a prayer that everyone in my audience opens their minds to my message. This is a very quiet and personal time. Unfortunately, this group had interrupted my mental "warm up" for the presentation. I was trying to concentrate. She also didn't realize that a motivator doesn't shout and jump around all the time he or she is off the stage. It is only when on the stage that you combine the power of your words with the power of an enthusiastic presentation.

Henry Chester defined enthusiasm as "faith in action." More than your dress, your body language or even the words on paper, your greatest asset will be your enthusiasm for the subject of your speech. Enthusiasm can be communicated in many ways. You don't have to jump around and shout to prove your commitment to an idea. You can be firm and steady, or soft and as quiet as a prayer and still communicate enthusiasm.

People believe in believers. When you demonstrate your beliefs through your enthusiastic presentation, people in the audience will naturally gravitate to your position. Enthusiasm is power. It is the energy that transforms a bland presentation into a powerful speech. It is the force that takes an intimidated speaker and turns him or her into a human dynamo. Enthusiasm provides the inspiration to change hearts and minds.

You can become an enthusiastic speaker. The effort will require discipline, nine disciplines to be precise. Master these and you can master any audience.

Discipline #1. Have an intent and act on it. Don't speak just to hear your own voice. Speak to persuade participants on your plan, to improve conditions for your co-workers, to motivate a positive change, to change the world.

Discipline #2. Realize your own power and responsibility for your own actions. You are your own man or woman. That realization brings responsibility, but also a remarkable sense of freedom.

Discipline #3. Stretch your limits. Each of us can do more than we believe possible. Imagine how enthusiastic you'll be when you break through those barriers.

Discipline #4. Accept yourself. Nobody's perfect and we all have room for improvement. As long as you continue to improve, don't knock yourself for today's errors. Learn from them and move on.

Discipline #5. Be true to yourself. Live and always be yourself when speaking. Don't try to imitate another. Live the life you know you were born to live.

Discipline #6. Allow enthusiasm to take over. When you feel enthusiasm racing through your system, run with it. Enthusiasm generates tremendous energy. Put it to work.

Discipline #7. Deliver the goods. The world is populated with just two types of people. Those who keep their promises and those who do not. Find a spot in the first group and nestle in for life. Your continuing positive lifestyle will manifest itself in an overriding enthusiasm.

Discipline #8. Be there! Focus on your audience and the needs of that audience. You have to be there 100%, regardless of whatever else may be going on in your life. Like a song or a poem, a speech is a process and you must enjoy that process. You must include highs and lows, rapid speech and slow, pauses and run-on sentences, and other techniques all designed to win over your audience and then motivate them. As they say in the entertainment business, the show must go on and you're the show.

Discipline #9. Paint word pictures. Speak from your heart while using your mind. Don't just talk about a product, service or an idea. Paint it with words. Involve all your audience's senses and allow them to mentally see, feel, touch, etc. As Captain Picard of the Starship Enterprise says, "Engage!"

> *"Enthusiasm is at the bottom of all progress. With it there is accomplishment. Without it there are only alibis."*
> Henry Ford

Exceed All Expectations

A great way to inspire an audience is to give them more than they expect. "Well, Omar, I'm already giving 100 percent. How can I do more?" you ask. It's all about expectations.

During the late 1960s President Johnson pulled himself out of the race for re-election. Popular thought says that he dropped out of the race after losing an important election primary to an under-funded, practically unknown Senator Eugene McCarthy. Here he was, the sitting President of the United States, elected by a landslide, and backed by the full power of the Democratic party, and yet he lost a primary he was supposed to win by an incredible margin of victory. As is so often the case, memory is selective. Johnson actually won that primary. The problem is that his margin of victory was slim when expectations were that he'd walk away with it. He actually came out on top in the primary election, but seemed the loser because of the expectations game. As they say, he "won the battle, but lost the war." You can set the expectations for your speech. And then you can exceed them. You can play the game and win. Don't make big promises, especially promises you can't possibly keep. Audiences are smart and they'll soon know whether or not you're living up to your promises. Simply tell your audience what you are about to do. Tell them your goals. Let them know the intent of your speech, the subject matter, and your qualifications. It's also a good idea to note the length of your presentation or the time that it will end. If the audience requests that you extend your presentation, in a Q&A session for example, that's fine. In fact, that's a great way to give more than you promise. Instead of promising the moon, take a lesson from Marc Antony's speech to the mob. "For I have neither wit, nor words, nor worth, action, nor utterance, nor the power of speech to serve men's blood..." A bit of self-deprecation early on can put the audience at ease and put them on your side. Then blow them away with your presentation. Give them more than they expect.

THE ONE-MINUTE SUMMARY

- Every speaker has a style. Your job is to create a great personal style to carry your words with passion.
- Generally, dress as your audience dresses.
- Speak with more than words. Learn and use body language as a visual aid to support your presentation.
- Make eye contact with various members of your audience, but don't focus exclusively on one person.
- Develop enthusiasm. It's contagious. Express it. Put it to use. Allow it to help win over your audience.
- The seven disciplines for developing enthusiasm are:
    - #1. Act with a purpose.
    - #2. Take responsibility for your own actions.
    - #3. Stretch your limits.
    - #4. Accept yourself.
    - #5. Be true to yourself.
    - #6. Allow enthusiasm to take over your life.
    - #7. Deliver the goods.
- Set your audience's expectations and then deliver more than you promise.

16

"The first and greatest commandment is, 'Don't let them scare you.'"

Elmer Davis

Controlling Your Fear Of Speaking

A wise man said, "The mind is a wonderful thing - it starts working the minute you're born and never stops until you get up to speak in public." It's natural to be afraid of speaking in public. Realize that. Accept it. And then move on. Knowing that you have that fear is essential in controlling it.

The fear of speaking never leaves you however, you can overcome and master that fear and turn yourself into a fearless speaker. I've spoken to more than 2,000,000 people and I still face the fear of speaking every time I face an audience. Here's why. My family fled Cuba when Castro and communism took over. I had been a pretty fair second grade student on that island where everybody spoke Spanish. Everybody in America spoke English and I didn't understand a word of the language, much less speak it. I was automatically placed in a kindergarten class for that reason. You can imagine what that demotion did for my self-image. I worked hard to learn my new language, which meant learning one word at a time. I had progressed so well that my kindergarten teacher asked me to make a speech at our cap and gown graduation. When I stepped up to make my speech I bowed to the applause from the audience. My cap fell off and as I bent over to pick it up my notes fell and scattered across the floor. I started talking, but without my notes and a solid command of English, I froze. Everyone started laughing and I ran out of the building. That day I promised myself I'd never speak before a crowd again.

Obviously I moved beyond that, but I still carry that fear with me to this day.

"But, Omar, you make your living speaking."

Yes, I do, but I do it by overcoming that fear. I keep reminding myself that I must have a purpose that is greater than the fear. I do it because the joy of helping others is far greater than my fear of speaking. That thought helps me overcome and master fear. You can break the fear barrier and overcome your fear of speaking, too. That's what this chapter is all about. The process is relatively simple:

- Know your subject
- Know yourself
- Gear Up.. Speak!

Let's take a look at each subject.

Periu's Point

Speaking skills develop daily, not in a day. If you've done everything I have discussed in this book up to this point, by now fear should be your ally. Think of it as rocket fuel to get you where you're going.

"If you gathered up all the fearful thoughts that exist in the mind of the average person, looked at them objectively, and tried to decide just how much good they provided that person, you would see that not some but all fearful thoughts are useless. They do no good. Zero. They interfere with dreams, hopes, desires, and progress."

Richard Carlson

I know about fear. I don't have your typical professional speaker's personality. I fight off the butterflies every time I step up on the stage. I take heart from one of the most used phrases in The Bible, "Fear not." That's good advice. Every time you step up, make your fear your ally. Use it to your advantage and speak without fear.

Know Your Subject

A business associate of mine has never delivered a "prepared speech" in his life, yet he has addressed audiences successfully for years. He has made the rounds on the circuit of business and community service clubs and has addressed crowds exceeding 300 in auditoriums and theaters. Two of those 300-member presentations were four hours in length in which his notes consisted only of a long list of words or short phrases. "How can you do that?," asked a friend. "Audiences can sense preparation and competence, or the lack of it. I just make sure I know my material inside and out. Everything flows naturally from that base of knowledge," he replied.

The fear of speaking before a group consistently leads the list of "greatest fears" every year. People fear public speaking more than they fear death. That's a proven fact and it's so unnecessary. The fear of speaking is often the fear of fouling up. It makes common sense that the more you know, the fewer mistakes you'll make. Study your subject. Read it. Think about it. Read supporting documents and think about them. Become even more of an expert and stay current on your area of expertise. Organize your thoughts. Write an outline or a series of notes on index cards. Play with the arrangement of materials until you have the ideal flow of information and documentation. Prepare your visual aids and make sure they match the topic being covered as you cover it. Again, think before you speak. Rehearse. Rehearse. Rehearse. The President's State of the Union message pretty much has to be delivered word for word from an extremely well-prepared document. You have a lot more flexibility. In most cases memorization or speaking from a script will detract from your speech. You'll seem less enthusiastic, less spontaneous, and less involved with your audience. Practice, practice and practice again. Once you're before that audience, the magic words will come.

You never get too old, too professional, or too practiced to not need rehearsal. I remember the first time I had dinner with Zig Ziglar. At the end of a pleasant meal he excused himself saying, "I have to go rehearse my speech for tomorrow morning." Wow! I thought to myself, this is a 76 year old man who is at the top of his profession. He's been speaking all his life and he's still rehearsing. Big wow! I asked him about it. Mr. Ziglar said that even though he's given a speech a thousand times, he likes to keep it fresh. "I rewrite my outline for every speech, even if I've given it a hundred times," he said. I've learned from the master and now I rewrite my outline every time I give a speech, too. That way it's always new for the audience - and for the speaker.

Rehearse your speech until you know it completely. There is no substitute for preparation. You want to be familiar and confident, but not mechanical. On-the-spot improvisation is fine provided any changes clarify your presentation and advance your intent.

"There are three things to aim at in public speaking; first to get into your subject, then to get your subject into yourself, and lastly, to get your subject into your hearers."

A.S. Gregg

"Be absolutely clear about the intent of your presentation. All else flows from that simple, powerful and necessary statement."

Omar Periu

Know Yourself

How do you react in those moments before your presentation?
- Rapid pulse rate?
- "Butterflies" in your stomach?
- Short, quick breaths?
- Sweaty palms?
- Quavering voice?
- Dry mouth?
- Slight sense of vertigo?
- A need to "toss your cookies?"
- Overriding desire to demonstrate your impression of the 100 meter dash?

Actually, that's all pretty good and useful information. Once you know the symptoms, you can begin to work on the disease. Believe me, I've felt all of those negative reactions (and a few more). Every time I get up to speak I'm still afraid I'll drop my graduation cap, spill my notes on the floor, and embarrass myself so much I'll run out the back door. The difference these days is that I take all that negative energy and turn it into a positive force to power a great presentation. You can do the same thing.

Knowing yourself and how you react before an audience is a blessing. You can't work on improving a technique if you are unaware of the problem. In that sense, nervousness is a very positive thing. If you know you have "butterflies" in your stomach, you can either let them flutter about until you're sick or you can find a butterfly net. I'll cover some of those "nets" in the next section.

Of course, there's an equally important part of knowing yourself - being yourself. Audiences can spot a phony and usually within the first moments of a presentation. They don't respond well to phoniness and, in fact, most of them will resent it. Be yourself, be fearless, and become a great speaker.

Gear Up

I've made more speeches and presentations than most of you folks, so I bet I've experienced a lot more of those butterflies. Here are a number of techniques for "netting" them that have worked well over the years.

Don't fight the feeling. If you're nervous, well, you're nervous. Accept that reality, but don't give in to it. Remember, fear can be a friend. There's a lot of energy in those feelings. Use them.

Take a walk. Naturally, you won't be in a position to walk around the block before every presentation, but opportunities will arise. Take advantage of them. Even inside a building you can often loosen up by walking around the halls.

Meditation. Even if you can't find a quiet moment in a quiet place before your presentation, you can find a quiet place within yourself. Meditation is simple and easily learned and you can even do it unnoticed with your eyes open in front of an audience.

Deep breathing is an excellent alternative. You'll be amazed at how calm you can become by taking a few slow and deep breaths. Breathe very deeply. Deep, low in the back breaths will relax you.

Isometric exercises pit one muscle group against another and you can do these anywhere, anytime. For example, the hands in prayer position, pushing against each other release and burn off a lot of excess nervousness. You can achieve the same effect by flexing your muscles. The effort has the added benefit of momentarily taking your mind off the speech.

Stretching. If you have the opportunity, run through a number of stretching exercises behind the curtain or in a private room before your presentation. They'll help drain some of your nervous energy and (literally) help you limber up for your speech.

Roll your shoulders. The human neck is a great storehouse of tension. Rolling your shoulders and gently rotating your neck releases that pent up energy.

Relax. I know, easier said than done, but it can be done. Relax every muscle in your body from head to toe or from toe to head. "My toes are relaxed...I feel my ankles relaxing...my knee joints relax..." This one's so easy you can do it while chit-chatting and pecking at your business lunch. You can also "send your mind" to any area of your body holding tension to tell that set of muscles to relax. It works.

Build pauses into your presentation. Too many speakers rush into speaking. They get so caught up in the process of "getting this thing over" that they continue the rush until the audience feels they are being run over. Pauses here and there allow you to catch your breath and assess your pacing. They give the audience a breather, too.

Knock on wood. We all have our own little rituals. Whether they are based in scientific reality or not is irrelevant. They make us feel better and feeling better enhances our performance. So, carry that rabbit's foot, snap your fingers three times, wear your lucky socks, or whisper the magic words. That's all part of how the magic happens.

Before I give a speech I always say a prayer that the participants will open their minds to my training, and that I am able to help them go for more choices. This simple and heartfelt ceremony helps me reduce fear and the wall between audience and speaker.

Periu's Point

Fear can be a speaker's friend. People automatically sense fear in another person. They know you're scared half out of your wits. They've all felt fear before and they're probably just as scared of public speaking as you are. That fact creates a sympathetic audience right from the beginning. In most cases, the audience is already on your side before you utter the first word. When you look out across your audience, you're seeing a group of people who admire and respect you for what you're doing.

Speak!

As you make more and more speeches, you'll develop your own style. Don't try to force the issue. It will evolve naturally if you follow the basics outlined here. You probably won't even know that you have developed a personal style until some appreciative member of the audience says so. As you confidently move forward, be aware of your progress. Don't allow speaking glitches to enter your speech patterns. Here are a few potential problems.

Poor or improper pronunciation of words is unforgivable. After all, it's your speech and you've had a lot of time to prepare it. Poor articulation of words and phrases is sloppy, shows a lack of respect for the audience, and leaves the impression that the speaker is less than knowledgeable or that he or she just doesn't care.

Mumbling, such as "uh...ah...er..." is a sign of nervousness, distraction, and lack of preparation. No one expects a speaker to deliver a perfect speech completely free of errors. The audience does expect at least, at a minimum, a competent speech that they can follow without a score card as to where the speaker is at the moment. Practice with a tape recorder or a friend to make sure you're free of these success killers.

Inappropriate or ill-timed gestures will confuse or even amuse (wrongly) your audience. Raising a hand upward fits nicely with "...as we reach for the stars." The same speech is diminished if the speaker steps forward with open arms pointing to the floor or sticks his hands into his pants pockets. Make sure your gestures match and enhance the words and don't make a gesture just to make a gesture. Avoid such annoying acts as drumming your fingers, rolling your eyes, jingling coins or keys in your pockets, or playing the drum solo from Benny Goodman's "Swing, Swing, Swing" with your pencils.

Upward inflection occurs when you ask a question and your voice goes up on the last word. That's fine for a question, but too many speakers slip up by accidentally using the same technique to turn a statement into a question and that dramatically weakens its impact.

Higher than normal voice pitch is the result of nervousness. The best way to prevent this is to practice deep breathing before you speak. Relax, you're good at this.

A nasal voice can result from a tightened jaw or by bunching your tongue at the back of your mouth. Awareness and relaxation are the keys to prevention. And if you're born with a naturally nasal voice, don't worry or be self-conscious. Many of the greatest speakers in the world have less than perfect voices. Some of the most famous stars of Broadway musicals can't really carry a tune, but they know how to "sell" a song. What really communicates is your passion for your subject and your commitment to your audience. Regardless, if the technical quality of your speaking voice, if you present passion and commitment, you will be a successful speaker.

Don't become obsessed with the thought of making a mistake. It's going to happen. I still blow a line now and then. Mistakes are part of the process. When you flub a line, mispronounce a word, or stumble in your presentation, just stop and correct the situation. Never apologize for or draw attention to an error. Simply restate what you meant to say correctly and then move on without additional comment.

Frank Tyger said, "Fear fades when facts are faced." Well, face these facts. You can become a fearless speaker. You can deliver with conviction, passion and your own winning personal style. Whenever those butterflies start fluttering remember that you are not alone. Every speaker who ever made a presentation has felt the same thing, including yours truly. Never take counsel of your fears. Listen to the passion in your heart and then speak.

Let me leave you with these words, it is an honor to speak before a group. It matters not whether that group is your co-workers, 10,000 people in a sports arena, or the assembled leaders of the Western World via satellite hookup. The speech is an honor. Honor yourself by honoring your audience. Knock them alive with your words. Spark their minds and bodies into action. Move their hearts and souls. Speak Without Fear.

> *"Half our fears are baseless; the other half discreditable."*
> Christian Bovee

THE ONE-MINUTE SUMMARY

- Every speaker experiences some fear of speaking. You're in good company.
- Control your fear by knowing your subject, knowing yourself, gearing up, focusing on your intent and actually making the speech.
- Know your subject through study, organization, and rehearsal. Knowledge helps stamp out fear.
- Understand your symptoms of fears so you can work on their cause.
- Techniques for gearing up include meditation, deep breathing, stretching, isometric exercises, taking a walk, rolling your shoulders, building pauses into your presentation, accepting your nervousness, and using personal ritual.
- Visualize a successful speech. Make it mind accomplished.
- Avoid mumbling, inappropriate or ill-timed gestures, a nasal voice, poor or improper word pronunciation, upward inflection on tatements, and a higher than normal voice pitch.

17

"Man is a tool-using animal...without tools he is nothing, with tools he is all."

Thomas Carlyle

Tools Of The Trade

Two young business executives were making an important presentation to the assembled U.S. and Canadian distributors of an industrial product. They were introducing the company's advertising and marketing program for the coming year and part of their program involved an automated slide show. A lot was on the line and their performance would affect the performance of the distribution network for the entire year.

The young speaker introduced his slide show. His associate punched the appropriate buttons, the lights dimmed, and the automated slide show began - two synchronized projectors timed perfectly with pre-recorded music and speech on tape. But the cues didn't cue up and slowly but steadily the audio began slipping away from the order of slides. The narration spoke of product B while the image was still on product A.

Working under controlled panic, the young man at the slide projector quickly grabbed a flashlight, a copy of the script and began to manually control the order of the projected images. He held the script in one hand and manipulated the machine with the other. The flashlight was crammed in his mouth. Within a few seconds sound and image were back in synch.

Then the flashlight batteries slowly died.

Luckily, the man running the projector was also the man who wrote the script and he was able to keep things pretty well on track.

Imagine the confusion if someone unfamiliar with the script had been running the equipment.

I've experienced just about every nightmare a meeting organizer and speaker can endure. I've been down the dark and dangerous roads some of you are just now entering. I hope you'll allow me to shed a little light on the subject. (Such as, always carry extra batteries.)

There is a variety of powerful tools of the trade at your disposal. I'll throw the spotlight on some of the most effective choices.

> *"Successful generals make plans to fit circumstances, but do not try to create circumstances to fit plans."*
> General George S. Patton, Jr.

> *"In other words, you have to be prepared to adjust your preparations. You have to be able to think on your feet and willing to act according to the new situation."*
> Omar Periu

Room With Your View

The first tool of the trade is your environment and there are three questions you must answer.

Question #1. Is the environment suitable? Does it fit your subject matter well? Will your audience be comfortable? Is it large or small enough? What are the likely distractions and how can you compensate for them? Will the environment overwhelm, "underwhelm," or draw attention from your presentation?

Question #2. Is the environment relevant to your subject matter? If you're speaking on poverty in the Third World, an elegant boardroom with leather chairs, mahogany paneling, and a sumptuously catered meal might send mixed messages. Of course, if you're seeking a budget increase, meeting in the dilapidated room with torn carpet, water stained ceiling, and peeling paint might reinforce your argument. What will best serve your needs?

Question #3. Will it work? Can everyone comfortably fit in? Will the traffic noise outside drown out your presentation for the folks in the back of the room? Can those folks see your visual aids from way back there? Will the room accommodate the seating arrangements you need? When I spoke at the Riviera penthouse in Las Vegas I couldn't help noticing the spectacular view of the city. The room holds 800 people and I didn't want to be addressing a large audience of people craning their necks for a better look at the neon rainbow outside. I closed the curtains so that their attention would be on the message and the messenger, not the light show down below.

Please note: You should ask these three questions about every tool you use:

- Is it suitable?
- Is it relevant?
- Will it work?

> *"One thing a speaker should remember for sure; The mind can absorb only what the seat can endure."*
> Maxwell Droke

Handouts Are Handy

Handouts can be used in a number of formats: copies of your speech, printed versions of your brochures or flyers specifically produced for your presentation, corporate brochures, or even product samples. Be careful with the latter. Handouts should enhance, not distract from your presentation.

If the handouts relate directly to your speech, present them prior to your presentation so the audience can follow what you are about to say. If the handout is a copy of your speech, material supporting but not directly following your speech, see that it is delivered at the end of the meeting.

Handouts work well with all sizes of audiences and can be used in any environment.

Propped Up

Props can be anything in three dimensions that your audience can look at, wander around, handle or pass along. A prop could be a model of the proposed building, a cutaway of the new engine, a symbol such as a small plastic pyramid standing in for the Great Pyramid, working models, or virtually any number of physical objects. If your meeting involves a plant tour, the entire facility is a prop.

Props actively engage not only the minds, but the senses of your audience. Plan your use of props to enhance the audience's appreciation of your intent.

It's Okay To Be Flip

One of the easiest tools to create and to use is the old fashioned flip chart. These tools can be professionally prepared with set type, colorful illustrations, and even photographs, or they can be made on the spot with a paper chart on an easel and an ink marker. Even hand-written charts can be prepared in advance. Some people lightly pencil-in their comments so that they can "write" them live, yet still be assured of neatness. Some presentations lend themselves to just scribbling the messages as you go.

Here are a few key considerations. Always keep a sheet of blank paper between each chart so there's no "bleed through." You don't want your audience to be one step ahead throughout the presentation. Keep your color scheme consistent. All headlines should be in one color, subheads in another, and text in another and follow this scheme throughout your speech. Remember that some people don't have 20/20 vision and those in the back rows who do still may have trouble seeing. Make your headlines at least three inches high, subheads two inches, and text at least one inch.

Flip charts are inexpensive, informal and are most useful in small groups.

Periu's Point

Murphy's Law states, "Everything is more complicated than it seems," and Mr. Murphy really knew his stuff. Whenever using presentation tools, bring extras of everything: extension cord, spare bulbs, spare batteries, color markers, acetate sheets, paper, video/audio tapes, pens, pencils, paper, whatever. Have a backup for everything or face another Murphy's Law - "The one thing you don't bring will be the one thing you need."

Overhead Projectors

Overhead projectors use transparent acetate sheets printed (or written) with text and/or graphics which are projected on a screen or even the wall. Often the speaker will write on the sheets as he or she makes the presentation. It's a good, efficient, inexpensive and easy technique.

Please don't make the mistake of using loose-leaf acetates. They are hard to control and have a tendency to slip and slide, especially when you try to write on one. A simple cardboard frame for each sheet will eliminate this problem. Be sure to number those frames or sheets so that you can restore order when the inevitable gust of wind from the opening door, blast from the open window or air circulation system sends your presentation flying across the floor.

If you're using the projector to highlight points of your speech, outline or use bullet points. Writing the entire presentation is impractical, extremely slow, hard to follow, and almost guaranteed to lose your audience.

Overhead projectors work well with small to medium size audiences.

Videotape

Video presentations are basically mini-movies involving sight, sound and "live" motion. They can involve on-camera narrators, facility walk-throughs, dramatic or comedic skits, product demonstrations, messages from key players in the organization, and any number of combinations of options. For example, an on-camera announcer leads into a dramatic skit illustrating a problem. He or she returns to show a product demonstration. This leads to another skit showing how the product has solved the problem in the real world which leads back to the on-camera announcer for an introduction to the president of the company for a wrap up and call to action. Of course, the same can be said for shooting and editing on film, although film is usually (not always) a more expensive and more complicated process. You can rent any number of generic videos or DVDs from various companies. Many of these are produced with extensive budgets, well-known personalities, and top quality production values. You can get a great production for a reasonable amount of money, "reasonable" being a relative term depending upon your budget. Other organizations want or need something that is specific to the company, service or need. They'll often produce their own video presentations in house or via an outside production company. Warning - I may have said mini-movie, but please don't get star struck. A video for a presentation is not a Hollywood movie. The person who decides to play producer or director in that frame of mind is asking for box office disaster. Think about the needs of your audience only and forget about winning the Oscar.

Presentation Software

The well-known product Power Point from Microsoft is an example of presentation software. The product lets the meeting manager/speaker prepare professional looking materials on his or her computer and incorporate them into a complete presentation. The end product can involve text, graphics, photography, video, film, sound, a variety of background colors, design elements, and even live linkup with the Internet. It's an exciting new tool.

Newness can be a handicap. Too many people in business latch on to new technology thinking that its use alone will guarantee success. Your speech still has to be well-planned, well-organized, and well-presented to achieve your goal. All the "whistles, buzzers and bells" in the world cannot disguise a bad presentation.

Presentation technology can be used on a small laptop computer or in a large room projected on a screen.

> *"Satinger's Law: It works better if you plug it in."*
> Arthur Bloch
>
> *"Regardless of the technological assets you use, it is your own enthusiasm, your ability to communicate, and motivational skills that provide the power for a great speech."*
> Omar Periu

New Technology, New Methods

The technological breakthroughs of recent years have created new ways to conduct meetings. Many of these new ways of doing business are replacing the traditional face-to-face get-togethers. Teleconferencing, video conferencing, and Internet conferencing are good examples. Some organizations are now conducting meetings that last for days or weeks via e-mail messages which are "scheduled" according to the varying and often conflicting schedules of the participants.

New options are available and newer ones are sure to come along. Don't be dazzled by new technology and don't incorporate it if there's no need. But realize that seemingly overwhelming problems in arranging a meeting (being on different continents and in different time zones, for example) may no longer be a problem at all. This is what Marshall Mcluhan meant when he wrote, "The new electronic interdependence recreates the world in the image of a global village."

When evaluating new technology, remember your good, old fashioned questions.

- Is it suitable?
- Is it relevant?
- Does it work?

THE ONE-MINUTE SUMMARY

- Before using any speaking "tools of the trade," ask: Is it suitable? Is it relevant? Does it work? Technology, even basic technology, can often get in the way of real communication.
- Speaking aids include handouts, props, flip charts, overhead projectors, videotape presentations, 35mm slide presentations, and presentation software. When planning your presentation evaluate which aid(s) is most appropriate. Don't use it simply because it is available.
- Don't incorporate any new technology simply because it is new. Everything involved in the presentation must be relevant to that presentation. Otherwise, the tools detract from achieving your intent.

Appendix A

Event Questionnaire

I. The Program
   A. What is the program theme?
      1. What is the purpose or mission?
      2. What does the theme mean to your group?
   B. What kind of meeting will this be (sales, educational, awards, annual, etc.)?
   C. What is the name and title of the introducer?
   D. What is the exact time of the presentation?
      1. Starting time
      2. Ending time
   E. What event(s) occurs before and after the presentation?
      1. Before
      2. After
   F. What is the role of the speaker in th everall program (opening, closing, keynote, etc.)
   G. Who, if any, are the other speakers and what are their topics?
   H. What did you specifically like or dislike about the previous speakers? Why? (Withhold names if you like, but comment on their work.)
   I. What ideas or skills do you want your group to learn from the presentation?
   J. Are there specific issues the speaker should address?
   K. How will you evaluate the success of the program when it is over?
II. Audience Analysis
   A. Audience
      1. Number attending?
      2. Are spouses invited?
      3. Percentage of males/females?
      4. Average age of the group?
      5. Range of ages?
      6. Educational background of audience?
      7. Average income level?

B. What are the job titles of those in the audience?

C. Will there be any people who do not fit the above descrip tion? Explain.

D. Are there any special people or guests in the audience? Who? Why?

E. Toward which group should the presentation primarily be addressed?

F. Describe the current attitude and spirit of:
   1. A typical member of the group.
   2. Your organization.
   3. Your industry.

G. What are the main opportunities/challenges currently facing your Organization?

III. Business Environment

A. How does your company generate new business? What percentage of the day is spent on generating new business vs. maintaining current accounts?

B. Who is your typical client (attendee)?

C. What is the average length of time from the point a customer is discovered until he or she accepts your product, service or idea?

D. Does an individual or a committee generally make decisions?

E. What are the most significant objections you/your organization faces?

F. What is the organizational structure of a leader's day? Any idea of a "day in the life" of one of your leaders?

G. Provide some input to develop 4-5 case studies of actual challenging experiences that can be used as a role plays/inter active group discussions to demonstrate the training concepts.

H. What is the most important outcome you want to see achieved as a result of this presentation/speech? What is the "big picture" goal?

I. Note any other outcome you see as important for the growth and development of your leaders

J. What is your industry?

K. What are the three key things the speaker should know about your group?

L. Are there any "buzzwords" (acronyms, industry slang, etc.) the speaker should know?

M. Is there a phrase or common saying that may be effectively used in the presentation?

N. Define your customer(s).

O. What kind of year did your group just have? What are your expectations for the upcoming year?

P. Are there any comments or information that would be helpful in tailoring this presentation for your group?

Q. Should the speaker have any problems/emergencies on the way to the presentation, who should be contacted?

IV. Contact Information

   A. Contactee

Name:	Office phone:
Address:	Home phone:
City:	Cell phone:
State/Zip:	E-mail:

   B. Exact Location for the Event

Name:	Direct phone:
Address:	Fax:
City:	Contact:
State/Zip:	

   C. Hotel Accommodations

Hotel name:	Direct phone:
Address:	Fax:
City:	Contact:
State/Zip:	

Will hotel reservations be made by your group or will the speaker be responsible?

V. Additional Information

   A. An agenda of the meeting.

   B. Relevant past meeting brochures/information.

   C. Any other information that may be helpful to the speaker.

Appendix B

I Am A Great Speaker!

This is my personal speaker's creed. I go over this form before every presentation. Feel free to use it to provide focus and to pump yourself up. It works

I. I Believe
    A. Why do I believe? (80%) My intent is _____.
    B. How do I believe? (20%) I am competent and capable.
II. External - (Be) 90% Passion. I entertain, educate and motivate. Internal - (In) 10% Logic. I don't forget the nuts 'n bolts of presentation.
III. See - Feel - Go
    A. I SEE my outline
    B. I FEEL my emotions. I connect with the emotions of the outline.
    C. I GO to give the speech.
    D. I IMAGINE what the audience will feel like when I complete my presentation.

> *"Congratulations, you've done the work, you've paid the price, it's magic time!!! Go and show the audience whether two, or 20,000 what you are made of."*
>
> Omar Periu

Appendix C
The Speaker's Creed

I am a speaker.

I am a great speaker getting better every time.

I am judged not by the apparent positive or negative response of my audience, but by the thoughts and actions of that audience following my presentation.

I do not fear failure, knowing that it is inevitable. Rather, I embrace all my speaking experiences knowing that every presentation is a learning experience.

I embrace speaking not only because it is personally satisfying, exciting and even fun, but because speaking is a way to contribute to the improvement of my world.

I am a fearless speaker

I SPEAK!

Omar Periu

INSURING CONTINUED SUCCESS

Since learning is an ongoing experience, I encourage you to continue your quest for success by investing in yourself and your business. Here's how...

• Request our catalog of audio, CD, and DVD programs designed to reinforce fundamentals and introduce innovative strategies that establish you as the recognized expert in your field. Make them an improtant piece of your business library.

• Inquire about my national and international public appearances, custom seminars and 2 and 3-day workshops, corporate presentations and ongoing training programs. My assistant will be happy to send you a schedule, additional information, or contact you in person to address your specific needs.

• Send your questions, observations, and personal accounts that occurred as a result of reading this book and adopting its principles on leadership. Who knows, perhaps you'll be a contributior to my next book.

OMAR PERIU

Omar Periu conducts sales training and motivational seminars nationally and internationally, specializing in:

- The One Minute Meeting
- Sales Training
- Sales Management Training
- Inspirational/Motivational Seminars
- Conventions
- Coaching and Mentoring programs
- Audio, CD, DVD Programs

If you want your next meeting or convention to be a guaranteed success and leave a lasting impression on your people, call now or write for a free consultation and more information:

Omar Periu International, Inc.

P. O. Box 812470

Boca Raton, FL 33481

888-777-4519

email: operiu@aol.com

www.OmarPeriu.com

To continue your personal and professional development, you will want to acquire more of *Omar Periu's Success* materials.

1. Sales Leadership Program

For over a decade Omar Periu has been known as the leading sales mangement authority. Mr. Periu has trained over two-thirds of the Fortune 500 sales managers. This program will teach you the qualities of superior leadership and how to manage yourself and others to obtain peak performace. Learn to act and achieve yor sales goals, improve your delagation and leadership skills, assemble a team with the "right stuff," and develop high impact, motivational techniques. (8 audio/16 sessions with interactive manual)

2. Investigative Selling Audio

Make the income you deserve! All sales masters understand and use these proven secrets of "Investigative Selling." In this 16-session, thought-provoking, audio program, Omar will teach you how to overcome fear, find and qualify clients, make dynamic presentations and dramatically increase your sales-closing ratio. (8 audio with interactive workbook)

3. Investigative Selling Book

Discover in this best-selling, "how to" book, the proven skills that will make your career skyrocket. Omar will teach you what he and countless other top producers and business owners know - how to turn "No's" into "Yes's." You'll learn the 12 Principles of Investigative Selling that made Omar a self-made multi-millionaire by the age of 31. This book is a must for any serious student of selling.

4. Awaken The Winner Within Audio

Omar Periu is synonymous with success. As a non-English speaking immigrant, Omar overcame the odds and created a life that most people only dream about. He knows what it takes to develop the success-building desire - a desire so intense and complete that it leads you to the secrets of greatness. (6 audio/12 sessions)

141

5. How To Master The Art of Effective Time Management

All highly paid sales executive know how to manage their time, their lives and their territories. In fact, effective time management is one of the highest paid skills in the world. In this audio series, Omar will teach you how to create a time-management plan that will work as hard as you do. He'll also teach you to organize, prioritize, overcome procrastination and set goals. Keep your career on track with effective time management skills. (6 audio/12 sessions)

6. Developing Power Prospecting Strategies To Get In

Learn how to prospect anyone, anywhere, amytime. Omar Periu is a successful public speaker, author, business owner, sales executive, writer, recording star, performer and above all, an exceptional teacher. He has made a lifetime career of helping people bring out the very best in themselves, their families, organi zations and communities. In this program, he will share with you the tools to become a champion prospector, a master at phone strategies - both hot and cold calling techniques. You'll learn effective networking strategies to build your business prospecting from the bottom up and get through back doors to the top VIP's of Fortune 500 companies. Experience how Omar will help you achieve success and greatness! (6 audio/12 sessions)

7. The Power of Motivation

How To Develop and Maintain A Positive Mental Attitude will help you to build a better self, team, and company through effective and innovative tech- niques. In this compelling program, Omar shares with you his "how to" ideas and proven principles that have enabled him to become a multi-millionaire. He presents inspiring stories and motivational concepts that will help you maxi- mize you and your team's future success. Upon completion of the program, you'll be encouraged to face your fears and kick your counter-productive habits. Enjoy the benefits of becoming a calculated risk taker; think about where you are now, where you want to be and how to reach success as quickly as possible. This is the ulimtate instruction course that will empower you and your people to handle rejection, remain slump-free, and capture the lion's share of the marketplace. (8 audio/6 sessions)

8. Health Is Wealth - How To Have The Energy To Succeed

By taking control of your life choices and learning how to master your habits, you can embark on your journey to personal fulfillment! Learn how to increase your capacity for stress by recapturing your energy. This program will be your tool to reaching new mental, physical and emotional heights. You'll soon realize the imortance of your daily decisions and how they impact your personal power to achieve top fitness. (6 audio/12 sessions)(6 audio/12 sessions)

9. Premeditated Success Audio

Premeditated Success, as simple-minded guide to health, wealth and happiness. Omar will share with you the "how to" principles that were taught to him by his mentor, Tom Murphy. Omar Periu and millions of others live a life in fear less pursuit of their dreams because of this outstanding goal-setting system created by Omar and his mentor, Tom. (8 audio/16 sessions and interactive workbook)

10. How To Raise Happy, Healthy and Successful Kids

This is a program designed to help parents discover the special skills that will help their child succeed in life. Learn what you can do to make your child a winner! A must for parents and grandparents who want to play an active role in helping their children develop healthy self-images, build family unity, nurture self-discipline, and rise above life's negative influences.

(6 audio/12 sessions)

11. The One Minute Meeting

Anyone in a leadership position needs to know how to create, develop and deliver a dynamic speech that motivates, entertains and educates. In Part One of this program you will learn how to conduct a great meeting, developing a meeting plan, managing your meeting, people problems or people opportunities and more. In Part Two, you will master the art of making a great speech, by analyzing yourself, your audience, outlining your presentation from A to Z, inspiring your audience, controlling your fear of speaking and much, much more.

12. Get Motivated

In a negative world, it is important to maintain your positive attitude and motivation, to stay on top of your game. Peak performers realize that to stay motivated, they need to look at new ways and create more habits that sustain motivating action. In this program, Omar will share with you his personal experiences, and life experiences of top achievers that stay motivated consistently, through good times and most importantly, in bad. By learning and applying the 101 lessons in this program, you will be energized and you will begin to see things in a different way. You will take action by discovering the traits, beliefs and practices of successful people in all walks of life. Learn how to wipe out worry, embrace change, build and manage success. Improve your relationships, live a motivated life, and much, much more.

Call for Additional Information
or a Free Product Catalog

Omar Periu International

P. O. Box 812470
Boca Raton, FL 33481
1-888-777-4519

www.omarperiu.com
Please visit our website to sign up for a weekly tip
and our free monthly newsletter.